P9-DFQ-691

Say It Right in GERMAN

**Easily Pronounced
Language Systems, Inc.**

INFINITE Destinations, ONE Pronunciation System

Mc
Graw
Hill

New York   Chicago   San Francisco   Lisbon   London   Madrid   Mexico City
Milan   New Delhi   San Juan   Seoul   Singapore   Sydney   Toronto

Library of Congress Cataloging-in-Publication Data

Say it right in German / Easily Pronounced Language Systems.
       p.   cm. — (Say it right)
    ISBN 0-07-146922-2
    1. German language—Spoken German.   2. German language—Pronunciation by foreign speakers.   3. German language—Conversation and phrase books—English.   I. Easily Pronounced Language Systems.   II. Say it right.

PF3121.S263   2006
438.3′421—dc 22   2006041873

3 4 5 6 7 8 9 10 11 12 13 14 15 16 17 18   LBM/LBM   0 9 8 7

ISBN-13: 978-0-07-146922-7
ISBN-10:   0-07-146922-2

McGraw-Hill books are available at special quantity discounts to use as premiums and sales promotions, or for use in corporate training programs. For more information, please write to the Director of Special Sales, Professional Publishing, McGraw-Hill, Two Penn Plaza, New York, NY 10121-2298. Or contact your local bookstore.

Also available:

Dígalo correctamente en inglés (Say It Right in English)
Say It Right in Chinese
Say It Right in French
Say It Right in Italian
Say It Right in Japanese
Say It Right in Spanish

Author: Clyde Peters
Illustrations: Luc Nisset

Acknowledgments

Betty Chapman, President, EPLS Corporation
Priscilla Leal Bailey, Senior Series Editor

This book is printed on acid-free paper.

CONTENTS

INTRODUCTION

The SAY IT RIGHT FOREIGN
LANGUAGE PHRASE BOOK
SERIES has been developed
with the conviction that learning to speak a foreign
language should be fun and easy!

All SAY IT RIGHT phrase books feature the EPLS
Vowel Symbol System, a revolutionary phonetic
system that stresses consistency, clarity, and above
all, simplicity!

Since this unique phonetic system is used in all
SAY IT RIGHT phrase books, you only have to
learn the VOWEL SYMBOL SYSTEM ONCE!

The SAY IT RIGHT series uses the easiest phrases
possible for English speakers to pronounce and
is designed to reflect how foreign languages are
used by native speakers.

You will be amazed at how confidence in your
pronunciation leads to an eagerness to talk to other
people in their own language.

Whether you want to learn a new language for
travel, education, business, study, or personal
enrichment, SAY IT RIGHT phrase books offer a
simple and effective method of pronunciation and
communication.

PRONUNCIATION GUIDE

Most English speakers are familiar with the German word **Danke**. This is how the correct pronunciation is represented in the EPLS Vowel Symbol System.

All German vowel sounds are assigned a specific non-changing symbol. When these symbols are used in conjunction with consonants and read normally, pronunciation of even the most difficult foreign word becomes incredibly EASY.

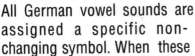

On the following page are all the EPLS Vowel Symbols used in this book. They are EASY to LEARN since their sounds are familiar. Beneath each symbol are three English words which contain the sound of the symbol.

Practice pronouncing the words under each symbol until you mentally associate the correct vowel sound with the correct symbol. Most symbols are pronounced the way they look!

THE SAME BASIC SYMBOLS ARE USED IN ALL SAY IT RIGHT PHRASE BOOKS!

EPLS VOWEL SYMBOL SYSTEM

Ⓐ

Ace
Bake
Safe

Ⓔ

See
Feet
Meet

Ⓘ

Ice
Kite
Pie

Ⓞ

Oak
Cold
Sold

ⓞⓞ

Cool
Pool
Too

ⓔ̆

Men
Red
Bed

ⓘ

Win
Give
if

ⓐⓗ

Mom
Hot
Off

ⓤⓗ

Sun
Fun
Run

Ⓤr

Hurt
Turn
Burn

ⓞⓤ

Could
Would
Book

ⓞⓨ

Toy
Boy
Joy

ⓞⓦ

Cow
How
Now

ⓔⓦ

New
Few
Dew

EPLS CONSONANTS

Consonants are letters like **T**, **D**, and **K**. They are easy to recognize and their pronunciation seldom changes. The following EPLS pronunciation guide letters represent some unique German consonant sounds.

Ķ   Represents a unique sound found inthe German letters **ch**. Pronounce the softest **k** sound possible. Very breathy. Have a German-speaking person pronounce these words for you.

   no**ch**   a**ch**

SH   These letters also represent another unique sound found in the German letters **ch**. You will naturally pronounce them like the **sh** in di**sh**. This is a good approximation but you must listen closely to a native speaker to master this unique German sound. Have a German speaker pronounce these words.

   ni**ch**t   i**ch**   mi**ch**

TS   Sounds like the **ts** in hi**ts**, but is often found at the beginning of a word.

ß   Represents a slightly rolled **r** sound.

PRONUNCIATION TIPS

- Each pronunciation guide word is broken into syllables. Read each word slowly, one syllable at a time, increasing speed as you become more familiar with the system.

- In German it is important to emphasize certain syllables. This mark (´) over the syllable reminds you to stress that syllable.

- Most of the symbols are pronounced the way they look!

- This phrase book provides a means to speak and be understood in German. To perfect your German accent you must listen closely to German speakers and adjust your speech accordingly.

- The pronunciation and word choices in this book were chosen for their simplicity and effectiveness.

- ß is the German character for ss.

- **BIT** is an abbreviation for **Bitte** which means "please" in German. You will see it used throughout the book.

ICONS USED IN
THIS BOOK

KEY WORDS

You will find this icon at the beginning of chapters indicating key words relating to chapter content. These are important words to become familiar with.

PHRASEMAKER

The Phrasemaker icon provides the traveler with a choice of phrases that allows the user to make his or her own sentences.

Say It Right in GERMAN

ESSENTIAL WORDS AND PHRASES

Here are some basic words and phrases that will help you express your needs and feelings in German.

Hello

Guten Tag

GOO-TEN TahK

How are you?

Wie geht es Ihnen?

VEE GAT ES EE-NEN

Fine / Very well

Sehr gut

ZER GOOT

And you?

Und Ihnen?

OUNT EE-NEN

Good-bye

Auf wiedersehen

OWF VEE-DUr-ZAN

Good morning

Guten Morgen

GOO-TĔN MOR-GĔN

Good evening

Guten Abend

GOO-TĔN ah-BĔND

Good night

Gute Nacht

GOO-Tuh Nahkt

Mr.

Herr

HĔR

Mrs.

Frau

FRow

Yes

Ja

Y@h

No

Nein

N①N

Please

Bitte

B①-T@h

Always remember to say **please** and **thank you**.

Thank you

Danke schön

D@hN-K@h SH@N

Excuse me

Entschuldigung

@NT-SH@L-D@-G@NG

I'm sorry

Es tut mir leid

@S T@T M@R L①D

I'm a tourist.

Ich bin ein Tourist.

ⒾSH BⒾN ⒾN TⓄⓄR-ⒾST

I do not speak German.

Ich spreche kein Deutsch.

ⒾSH SHPRⒺ-SHⓊ KⒾN DⓄYTCH

I speak a little German.

Ich spreche etwas Deutsch.

ⒾSH SHPRⒺ-SHⓊ ⒺT-VⒶS DⓄYTCH

Do you understand English?

Verstehen Sie Englisch?

FⒺR-SHTⒶ-ⒺN ZⒺ ⒺN-GLⒾSH

I don't understand!

Ich verstehe nicht!

ⒾSH FⒺR-SHTⒶ-Ⓤ NⒾSHT

Please repeat.

Wiederholen Sie bitte.

VⒺ-DⓊR-HⓄ-LⒺN ZⒺ BⒾ-TⓊ

FEELINGS

I want...

Ich möchte...

Ⓘˢᴴ MⓊⓇ́ˢᴴ-Tⓤⓗ...

I have...

Ich habe...

Ⓘˢᴴ Hⓐⓗ́-Bⓤⓗ...

I know.

Ich weiß es.

Ⓘˢᴴ VⒾS ⓔˢS

I don't know.

Ich weiß nicht.

Ⓘˢᴴ VⒾS NⒾˢᴴT

I like it.

Es gefällt mir.

ⓔˢS Gⓔ́-Fⓔ́LT MⒺⒺR

I don't like it.

Es gefällt mir nicht.

ⓔˢS Gⓔ́-Fⓔ́LT MⒺⒺR NⒾˢᴴT

I'm lost.

Ich habe mich verlaufen.

ISH Hah-Buh MiSH FeR-Low-feN

I'm in a hurry.

Ich habe es eilig.

ISH Hah-Buh eS I-LiG

I'm tired.

Ich bin müde.

ISH BiN Mew-Duh

I'm ill.

Ich bin krank.

ISH BiN KRahNK

I'm hungry.

Ich habe Hunger.

ISH Hah-Buh HooN-GUr

I'm thirsty.

Ich habe Durst.

ISH Hah-Buh DooRST

I'm angry.

Ich bin böse!

ISH BiN BUr-Zuh

INTRODUCTIONS

My name is...

Ich heiße...

ⓘ<u>SH</u> Hⓘ-S⬭...

What's your name?

Wie heißen Sie?

Vⓔⓔ Hⓘ-Sⓔ̱N Zⓔⓔ

Where are you from?

Woher sind Sie ?

Vⓞ́-Hⓔ̱R Zⓘ NT Zⓔⓔ

Do you live here?

Wohnen Sie hier?

Vⓞ́-Nⓔ̱N Zⓔⓔ HⓔⓔR

I just arrived.

Ich bin erst angekommen.

ⓘ<u>SH</u> BⓘN ⓔ̱RST ⓐⁿN-Gⓤⓗ-Kⓞ-Mⓔ̱N

What hotel are you (staying) at?

In welchem Hotel sind Sie?

ⓘN Vⓔ̱L-<u>SH</u>ⓔ̱M Hⓞ-Tⓔ̱L Zⓘ NT Zⓔⓔ

I'm at the...hotel.

Ich bin im Hotel....

Ⓘ^{SH} BⓘN ⓘM HⓄ-TⓔL...

It was nice to meet you.

Nett Sie kennenzulernen.

NⓔT ZⒺ KⓔN-NⓔN-TSⓄⓄ-LⓔR-NⓔN

See you tomorrow.

Bis morgen.

BⓘS MⓄR-GⓔN

See you later.

Bis später.

BⓘS SHPⒶ-TⓊʳ

Good luck!

Viel Glück!

FⒺL GLⓔⓌK

THE BIG QUESTIONS

Who?

Wer?

VⓔR

Who is it?

Wer ist das?

VⓔR ⒤ST DⓐⓗS

What?

Was?

VⓐⓗS

What's that?

Was ist das?

VⓐⓗS ⒤ST DⓐⓗS

When?

Wann?

VⓐⓗN

Where?

Wo?

VⓄ

Where is...?

Wo ist...?

VO OST

Which?

Welch?

VÉL SH

Why?

Warum?

Vah-ROOM

How?

Wie?

VEE

How much? (money)

Wieviel?

VEE-FEEL

How long?

Wie lang?

VEE LahNG

ASKING FOR THINGS

The following phrases are valuable for directions, food, help, etc.

I would like...

Ich möchte...

Ⓘ^{SH} MⓊ^{SH}-Tⓤⓗ...

I need...

Ich brauche...

Ⓘ^{SH} BRⓞⓦ-Ⓚⓤⓗ...

Can you...?

Können Sie...?

KⓊ-Nⓔ̃N Zⓔⓔ...

When asking for things be sure to say <u>please</u> and <u>thank you</u>.

Please	**Thank you**
Bitte	Danke schön
Bⓘ-Tⓤⓗ	Dⓐ̈N-Kⓤⓗ SHⓊN

PHRASEMAKER

Combine **I would like** with the
following phrases beneath, and
you will have a good idea how to ask for things.

I would like...

Ich möchte...

(i)ᔆᴴ MⓊᵣᔆᴴ-Tⓤₕ... BIT

▶ **more coffee**

mehr Kaffee

MⓔR Kⓐₕ-FⒶ

▶ **some water**

etwas Wasser

ⓔT-VⓐₕS Vⓐₕ-SⓊᵣ

▶ **some ice**

etwas Eis

ⓔT-VⓐₕS (i)S

▶ **the menu**

die Speisekarte

DⒺ SHP(i)-Zⓤₕ-KⓐₕR-Tⓤₕ

PHRASEMAKER

Here are a few sentences you can
use when you feel the urge to say
I need… or **Can you**…?

I need...

Ich brauche…

①ᔆᴴ BR⓪-Kⓤ…

▶ **help**

Hilfe

H©L-Fⓤ

▶ **directions**

Richtungen

R①ᔆᴴ-T⓪NG-©N

▶ **more money**

mehr Geld

M©R G©LD

▶ **change**

Kleingeld

KL①N-G©LD

▶ **a lawyer**

einen Rechtsanwalt

①-N©N R©ᔆᴴTS-@N-V@LT

PHRASEMAKER

Can you...
Können Sie...
KÜ-NⓔN ZⒺⒺ...BIT

▶ **help me?**
mir helfen?
MⒺⒺR HⓔL-FⓔN

▶ **show me?**
mir zeigen?
MⒺⒺR TSⒾ-GⓔN

▶ **give me...?**
mir...geben?
MⒺⒺR...GⒶ-BⓔN

▶ **tell me...?**
mir sagen...?
MⒺⒺR SⒶ-GⓔN

▶ **drive me to...?**
fahren Sie mich zum...?
Fⓐ-RⓔN ZⒺⒺ MⒾ^SH TSⓄⓄM...

ASKING THE WAY

No matter how independent
you are, sooner or later you'll
probably have to ask for
directions.

Where ist...?

Wo ist...?

V⓪ ①ST...

Is it near?

Ist es in der Nähe?

①ST ⓔS ①N DⓔR N⦿́-ⓤ

Is it far?

Ist es weit?

①ST ⓔS V①T

I'm lost!

Ich habe mich verlaufen!

①ᔆᴴ Hⓐ-Bⓤ M①ᔆᴴ FⓔR-Lⓞ-Fⓔ N

I'm looking for...

Ich suche nach...

①ᔆᴴ Zⓞⓞ-Ҟⓤ Nⓐᛕ...

PHRASEMAKER

Where is...

Wo ist...

VO OIST...

▶ **the restroom?**

die Toilette?

DEE TWah-LÉ-Tuh

▶ **the telephone?**

das Telefon?

Dah S TÉ-LÉ-FON

▶ **the beach?**

der Strand?

DéR SHTRahNT

▶ **the hotel?**

das Hotel?

Dah S HO-TÉL

▶ **the train for...?**

der Zug nach...?

DéR TSooK Nah K...

TIME

What time is it?

Wieviel Uhr ist es?

VEE-FEL OOR IST ES

Morning

der Morgen

DER MOR-GEN

Noon

der Mittag

DER MI-TahG

Night

der Nacht

DER NahKT

Today

Heute

Hoy-Tuh

Tomorrow

Morgen

MOR-GEN

This week

Diese Woche

DEE-Zuh VO-Kuh

This month

Diesen Monat

DEE-ZěN MO-NahT

This year

Dieses Jahr

DEE-ZěS YahR

Now

Jetzt

YěTST

Soon

Bald

BahLT

Later

Später

SHPA-TUr

Never

Nie

NEE

WHO IS IT?

I
Ich
Ⓘ‵ᔕᴴ

You
Sie
Zⓔⓔ

We	**They**
Wir	Sie
VⓔⓔR	Zⓔⓔ

Him	**Her**
Ihn	Sie
ⓔⓔN	Zⓔⓔ

THE, A (AN), AND SOME

To use the correct form of **The, A (An)**, or **Some**, you must know if the German word is masculine, feminine, or neuter. Often you will have to guess! If you make a mistake, you will still be understood.

The

Die

D(EE)

The before feminine nouns (die) women are pretty.

Der

D(ê)R

The before masculine.. nouns: (der) men are handsome.

Das

D(ah)S

The before neuter nouns: (**das**) child is cute.

Die

D(EE)

The in front of plural nouns of all three genders:
(**die**) children are cute.

A or An

Ein

(I)N

A or **an** before masculine and neuter nouns:
He is (**ein**) man.

Eine

(I)́-N(uh)

A or **an** before feminine nouns:
She is (**eine**) woman.

Some

Eine

(I)́-N(uh)

USEFUL OPPOSITES

Near	**Far**
Nähe	Weit entfernt
N(A)́-(uh)	V(I)T (e)́NT-F(e)́RNT

Here	**There**
Hier	Dort
H(EE)R	D(ah)RT

Left	**Right**
Links	Rechts
L(EE)NKS	R(e)́(SH)TS

A little	**A lot**
Ein bisschen	Viel
(I)N B(I)́S-SH(e)́N	F(EE)L

More	**Less**
Mehr	Weniger
M(e)́R	V(A)́-N(I)-G(Ur)

Big	**Small**
Groß	Klein
GR(O)S	KL(I)N

Open	**Closed**
Offen	Geschlossen
Ō-FĒN	GĒ-SHLŌ-SĒN

Cheap	**Expensive**
Billig	Teuer
BĪ-LĪG	TOY-Ur

Clean	**Dirty**
Rein	Schmutzig
RĪN	SHMOO-TSĪG

Good	**Bad**
Gut	Schlecht
GOOT	SHLĒ-SHT

Vacant	**Occupied**
Frei	Besetzt
FRĪ	BĒ-ZĒTST

Right	**Wrong**
Richtig	Falsch
RĪSH-TĪG	FahLSH

WORDS OF ENDEARMENT

I love you.

Ich liebe dich.

(i)ᔆᴴ LⒺⒺ'-Bⓤⓗ D(i)ᔆᴴ

My love.

Meine Liebe. (f)   Mein Lieber. (m)

M(i)'-Nⓤⓗ LⒺⒺ'-Bⓤⓗ   M(i)'N LⒺⒺ'-BⒺⓇ

My life

Mein Leben

M(i)N LⒶ'-BⒺN

My friend (to a male)

Mein Freund (male)

M(i)N FRⓞⓥNT

My friend (to a female)

Meine Freundin

M(i)'-Nⓤⓗ FRⓞⓥN-D(i)N

Kiss me!

Küß mich!

KⓞⓤS M(i)ᔆᴴ

WORDS OF ANGER

What do you want?

Was möchten Sie?

VⓐS MⓊ'ˢᴴ-TⓔN Zⓔⓔ

Leave me alone!

Lassen Sie mich in Ruhe!

Lⓐ'-SⓔN Zⓔⓔ MⒾˢᴴ ⓘN Rⓞⓞ-Hⓔ

Go away!

Gehen Sie weg!

Gⓐ'-ⓔN Zⓔⓔ VⓔK

Stop bothering me!

Hören Sie auf!

HⓊ'-ⓔN Zⓔⓔ ⓞⓦF

Be quiet!

Sei still!

SⒾN Zⓔⓔ ˢᴴTⓘL

That's enough!

Das ist genug!

DⓐS ⓘST Gⓔ'-NⓞⓞK

COMMON EXPRESSIONS

When you are at a loss for words but have the feeling you should say something, try one of these!

Who knows?

Wer weiß es?

VⒺR VⒾS ⒺS

That's the truth!

Das ist die Wahrheit!

DⓐS ⓘST DⒺⒺ VⓐʾR-HⒾT

Sure!

Doch!

DⓄK

What's happening?

Was ist los?

VⓐS ⓘST LⓄS

I think so.

Ich glaube das.

ⓘSH GLⓄⓌ-Bⓤh DⓐS

Cheers!

Prosit!

PRŌ-ZĪT

Good luck!

Viel Glück!

FEEL GLewK

With pleasure!

Es freut mich!

ĕS FRoyT MĪSH

My goodness!

Ach du lieber!

ahK Doo LEE-Buh

What a shame! / That's too bad.

Das ist Schade.

DahS ĪST SHah-Duh

Well done!	**Bravo!**
Gut gemacht!	Bravo!
Goot Gĕ-MahKT	BRah-VŌ

Never mind.

Macht nichts .

MahKT NĪSHTZ

USEFUL COMMANDS

Stop!
Halt!
H@LT

Go!
Geh!
G@

Wait!
Warte!
V@R-T@

Hurry!
Schnell!
SHN@L

Slow down!
Langsam!
L@NK-S@M

Come here!
Kommen Sie hier, bitte!
K@-M@N Z@ H@R BIT

Help!
Hilfe!
H@L-F@

EMERGENCIES

Fire!

Feuer!

F@y'-@r

Emergency!

Ein Notfall!

@N N@T'-F@L

Call the police!

Rufen Sie die Polizei!

R@-F@N Z@ D@ P@-L@-TS@

Call a doctor!

Rufen Sie einen Arzt!

R@-F@N Z@ @-N@N @RTST

Call an ambulance!

Lassen Sie einen Krankenwagen kommen!

L@'-S@N Z@ @-N@N

KR@NK-@N-V@-G@N K@'-M@N

I need help!

Ich brauche Hilfe!

@^SH BR@'-K@ H@L-F@

ARRIVAL

Passing through customs should be easy since there are usually agents available who speak English. You may be asked how long you intend to stay and if you have anything to declare.

- Have your passport ready.

- Be sure all documents are up-to-date.

- While in a foreign country, it is wise to keep receipts for everything you buy.

- Be aware that many countries will charge a departure tax when you leave. Your travel agent should be able to find out if this affects you.

- If you have connecting flights, be sure to reconfirm them in advance.

- Make sure your luggage is clearly marked inside and out.

- Take valuables and medicines in carry-on bags.

SIGNS TO LOOK FOR:

GRENZE (Border)

ZOLL (Customs)

GEPÄCK (Baggage Claim)

KEY WORDS

Baggage

Gepäck

GĔ-PĔK

Customs

Zoll

TSOL

Documents

Papiere

Pⓐ-PEE-Ruh

Passport

Paß

PⓐS

Porter

Gepäckträger

GĔ-PĔK-TRⒶ-GUr

Tax

Steuer

SHToy-Ur

USEFUL PHRASES

Here is my passport.

Hier ist mein Paß.

HⒺR ①ST M①N PⓐS

I have nothing to declare.

Ich habe nichts zu erklaren.

①ˢᴴ Hⓐ-Ⓑⓤ N①ˢᴴT
TS⊚ ⓔR-KLⓔR-ⓔN

I'm here on business.

Ich bin hier auf Geschäft.

①ˢᴴ B①N HⒺR ⓸F Gⓔ-SHⓔFT

I'm here on vacation.

Ich bin hier in Ferien.

①ˢᴴ B①N HⒺR ①N FⒺR-Ⓔ-ⓔN

Is there a problem?

Gibt es ein Problem?

GⒺPT ⓔS ①N PRⓄ-BLⓐM

PHRASEMAKER

I'll be staying...

Ich bleibe...

ⒾSH BLⒾ-Bⓤⓗ...

▶ **one week**

eine Woche

Ⓘ-Nⓤⓗ VⓄ-Kⓤⓗ

▶ **two weeks**

zwei Wochen

TSVⓘ VⓄ-Kⓔⓝ

▶ **one month**

einen Monat

Ⓘ-Nⓔⓝ MⓄ-NⓐⓗT

▶ **two months**

zwei Monate

TSVⓘ MⓄ-Nⓐⓗ-Tⓤⓗ

USEFUL PHRASES

I need a porter!

Ich brauche einen Gepäckträger!

ⒾSH BRⓞⓦ-Ⓚⓤⓗ ⓘ-NⒺN

GⒺ-PⒺK-TRⒶ-GⓊⓇ

These are my bags.

Das ist mein Gepäck.

DⓐⓢS ⓘST MⓘN GⒺ-PⒺK

I'm missing a bag.

Es fehlt einen Koffer.

ⒺS FⒺLT ⓘ-NⒺN KⓄ-FⓊⓇ

Take my bags to a taxi, please.

Nehmen Sie meinen Koffer zum Taxi, bitte.

NⒶ-MⒺN ZⒺⒺ Mⓘ-NⒺN KⓄ-FⓊⓇ

ZⓄⓤM TⓐⓗK-SⒺⒺ BIT

Thank you. This is for you.

Danke schön. Das ist für Sie.

DⓐⓗN-Ⓚⓤⓗ SHⓊN

DⓐⓢS ⓘST FⒺⓦR ZⒺⒺ

PHRASEMAKER

Where is...

Wo ist...

VŌ ĬST...

▸ **customs?**

der Zoll?

DĔR TSŌL

▸ **baggage claim?**

die Gepäckausgabe?

DĒ GĔ-PĔK-ⓞⓦS-Gⓐ̄-Bⓤ̆

▸ **the money exchange?**

die Wechselstube?

DĒ VĔK-SŌ̆L-SHTⓞⓞ-Bⓤ̆

▸ **the taxi stand?**

der Taxistand?

DĔR Tⓐ̆K-SĒ-SHTⓐ̆NT

▸ **the bus stop?**

die Bushaltestelle?

DĒ BⓞⓤS-Hⓐ̆L-Tⓤ̆-SHTĔ-Lⓤ̆

HOTEL SURVIVAL

A wide selection of accommodations, ranging from the most basic to the most extravagant, are available wherever you travel in Germany. When booking your room, find out what amenities are included for the price you pay.

- Make reservations well in advance and get written confirmation of your reservations before you leave home.

- Always have identification ready when checking in.

- Do not leave valuables, prescriptions, or cash in your room when you are not there!

- Electrical items like blow-dryers may need an adapter. Your hotel may be able to provide one, but to be safe, take one with you.

KEY WORDS

Hotel

Hotel

HO-TĕL

Bellman

Hoteldiener

HO-TĕL-DĒ-NUr

Maid

Zimmermädchen

TSĪ-MUr-MAD-CHĕN

Message

Nachricht

NahK-RĪ-SHT

Reservation

Reservierung

Rĕ-ZĕR-VĒR-OONG

Room service

Hausdiener

HOWS-DĒ-NUr

CHECKING IN

RECEPTION

My name is...

Ich heiße...

(i)ᔆᴴ H(i)́-S(uh)...

I have a reservation.

Ich habe eine Reservierung.

(i)ᔆᴴ H(ah)-B(uh) (i)́-N(uh)

R(ē)-Z(ē)R-V(ee)́R-(ou)NG

Have you any vacancies?

Haben Sie ein Zimmer frei?

H(ah)́-B(ē)N Z(ee) (i)N TS(i)́-M(ur) FR(i)

What is the charge per night?

Wieviel kostet es pro Nacht?

V(ee)́-F(ee)L K(o)́S-T(ē)T (ē)S PR(o) N(ah)KT

Is there room service?

Gibt es Zimmerservice?

G(ee)PT (ē)S TS(i)́-M(ur)-S(ē)R-V(i)S

PHRASEMAKER

I would like a room ...

Ich möchte ein Zimmer...

Ī͞SH MŪ͡SH-Tᵘʰ ĪN TSĪ-MŪr...

▸ **with a bath**

mit einem Bad

MĪT Ī-NᵉM BᵃʰT

▸ **with one bed**

mit einem Bett

MĪT Ī-NᵉM BᵉT

▸ **with two beds**

mit zwei Betten

MĪT TSVĪ Bᵉ-TᵉN

▸ **with a shower**

mit einer Dusche

MĪT Ī-NŪr D͞OOSH-ᵘʰ

▸ **with a view**

mit einem Aussicht

MĪT Ī-NᵉM ᴼᵂS-SĪSHT

USEFUL PHRASES

Where is the dining room?

Wo ist der Speisesaal?

V◎ ①ST D⑥R SHP①-Z⑩-Z⑩L

Are meals included?

Ist das Essen inbegriffen?

①ST D⑩S ⑥S-⑥N ①N-B⑥-GR①-F⑥N

What time is breakfast?

Wieviel Uhr gibt es Frühstück?

V⑥-F⑥L ⑩R G⑥PT ⑥S
FR⑥-SHT⑩K

What time is lunch?

Wieviel Uhr gibt es Mittagessen?

V⑥-F⑥L ⑩R G⑥PT ⑥S
M①-T⑩K-⑥S-⑥N

What time is dinner?

Wieviel Uhr gibt es Abendessen?

V⑥-F⑥L ⑩R G⑥PT ⑥S
⑩-B⑥NT-⑥S-⑥N

My room key, please.

Mein Zimmerschlüssel, bitte.

MⒾN TSⒾ-MⓊr-SHLⓔw-SⓔL BIT

Are there any messages for me?

Gibt es eine Botschaft für mich?

GⒺPT ⒺS Ⓘ-Nⓤh
BⓄT-SHⓐFT FⓔwR MⒾSH

Please wake me at...

Bitte wecken Sie mich um...

BⒾ-Tⓤh VⒺK-ⒺN ZⒺ MⒾSH ⓄⓄM...

6:00	6:30
sechs	halb sieben
ZⒺKS	HⓐLP ZⒺ-BⒺN

7:00	7:30
sieben	halb acht
ZⒺ-BⒺN	HⓐLP ⓐKT

8:00	8:30
acht	halb neun
ⓐKT	HⓐLP NⓄⓎN

9:00	9:30
neun	halb zehn
NⓄⓎN	HⓐLP TSⓐN

PHRASEMAKER

I need...

Ich brauche...

Ⓘ^{SH} BRⓞⓦ-Ⓚⓤⓗ... BIT

▸ **a babysitter**

einen Babysitter

Ⓘ-NⓔN BⒶ-BⒺⒺ-SⒾ-TⓊr

▸ **bellman**

der Hoteldiener

DⒺⒺR HⓄ-TⓔL-DⒺⒺ-NⓊr

▸ **more blankets**

noch Decken

NⓄK DⓔK-ⓔN

▸ **a hotel safe**

einen Tresor

Ⓘ-NⓔN TRⓔ-ZⓄR

▸ **ice cubes**

Eiswürfel

ⒾS-VⓔⓦR-FⓔL

▶ **an extra key**

einen extra Schlüssel

Ī-NⓔN ⓔKS-TRⓊⓗ SHLⓔⓦ-SⓔL

▶ **a maid**

das Zimmermädchen

DⓐⓗS TSĪ-MⓊⓡ-MⓐD-CHⓔN

▶ **the manager**

den Manager

DⓔN Mⓐⓗ-Nⓔ-JⓊⓡ

▶ **clean sheets**

das saubere Bettwäsche

DⓐⓗS Zⓞⓦ-BRⓔ BⓔT-Vⓔ-SHⓔ

▶ **soap**

Seife

ZĪ-FⓊⓗ

▶ **toilet paper**

Toilettenpapier

TWⓐⓗ-LⓔT-ⓔN Pⓐⓗ-PⒺⒺR

▶ **more towels**

mehr Handtücher

MⓔR HⓐⓗNT-Tⓔⓦ-SHⓊⓡ

PHRASEMAKER

(PROBLEMS)

There is ...

Es gibt ...

ⓔS GⒺⒺPT...

▶ **no electricity**

keine Elektrizität

KⒾ-Nⓤ ⓔ-LⓔK-TRⒺⒺ-TSⒺⒺ-Tⓐ́T

▶ **no heat**

keine Heizung

KⒾ-Nⓤ HⒾ́-TSⓞNG

▶ **no hot water**

kein heisses Wasser

KⒾN HⒾ́-Sⓔ̲S Vⓐ́-SⓊ

▶ **no light**

kein Licht

KⒾN LⒾT

▶ **no toilet paper**

kein Toilettenpapier

KⒾN TWⓐ-Lⓔ́T-ⓔ̲N-Pⓐ-PⒺⒺR

PHRASEMAKER
(SPECIAL NEEDS)

Do you have...

Haben Sie...

H@h-B@N Z@...

▶ **an elevator?**

einen Aufzug?

@-N@N @F-TS@K

▶ **a ramp?**

eine Rampe?

@-N@ R@MP-@

▶ **a wheelchair?**

einen Rollstuhl?

@-N@N R@L-SHT@L

▶ **facilities for the disabled?**

Einrichtungen für Behinderte?

@N-R@SH-T@NG-@N F@R
B@-H@N-D@r-T@

CHECKING OUT

The bill, please.

Die Rechnung, bitte.

DEE REESH-NooNG BIT

Is this bill correct?

Ist diese Rechnung richtig?

IST DEE-Zuh REESH-NooNG RISH-TIG

Do you accept credit cards?

Nehmen Sie Kreditkarten an?

NAH-MEN ZEE KREE-DEET-KahR-TEN ahN

Could you have my luggage brought down?

Können Sie bitte mein Gepäck hierher
bringen lassen?

KUr-NEN ZEE BI-Tuh MIN
GEE-PEK HEER-HER BREENG-EN
Lah-SEN

Can you call a taxi for me?

Können Sie mir ein Taxi anrufen?

KÜ-NŎN ZEE MEER ĬN TahK-SEE
ahN-ROO-FŎN BIT

I had a very good time!

Ich habe viel Spaß gehabt!

ĬSH Hah-Buh FEEL SHPahS GĔ-HahPT

Thanks for everything.

Vielen Dank.

FEE-LŎN DahNK

I'll see you next time.

Bis nächstes Mal.

BĬS NĔKS-TĔS MahL

Good-bye

Auf Wiedersehen

OWF VEE-DŬr-ZAhN

RESTAURANT SURVIVAL

In Germany you will find a wide variety of foreign cuisines to choose from, as well as unpretentious regional fare and elegant haute cuisine.

- Breakfast, **Frühstück,** is usually served at your hotel. Lunch, **Mittagessen,** is normally served from noon to 2:30 PM. It is considered the main meal of the day. Dinner, **Abendessen,** from 6 PM to 9 PM.

- Menus are posted outside eating establishments and may contain the following statement: **Bedienung inbegriffen**, which means "service included."

- In restaurants it is customary to share a table that has empty seats. The exception is fine dining where tables that have a sign that says **Stammtisch** are reserved.

- Dining in Germany is considered an experience not to be rushed. Additionally, many items on the menu are made after you order.

KEY WORDS

Breakfast

Frühstück

FR**ew**-SHT**ou**K

Lunch

Mittagessen

M**i**-T**ah**K-**e**S-**e**N

Dinner

Abendessen

ah-B**e**NT-**e**S-**e**N

Waiter

Kellner

K**e**L-N**ur**

Waitress

Kellnerin

K**e**L-N**ur**-**i**N

Restaurant

Restaurant

R**e**S-T**o**-R**ah**NT

USEFUL PHRASES

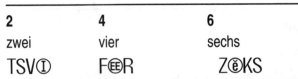

A table for...

Einen Tisch für...

ÏN-ẽN TÏSH FewR...

2	4	6
zwei	vier	sechs
TSVÏ	FEER	ZẽKS

The menu, please.

Die Speisekarte, bitte.

DEE SHPÏ-Zuh-Kahr-Tuh BIT

Separate checks, please.

Getrennte Bezahlung, bitte.

Gẽ-TRẽN-Tuh Bẽ-TSah-LouNG BIT

We are in a hurry.

Wir haben es eilig.

VEER Hah-Bẽn ẽS Ï-LÏG

What do you recommend?

Was empfehlen Sie?

Vah S ẽMP-Fa-Lẽn ZEE

Please bring me...

Bringen Sie mir... bitte

BR**EE**NG-**ê**N Z**EE** M**EE**R... BIT

Please bring us...

Bringen Sie uns... bitte

BR**EE**NG-**ê**N Z**EE** **ou**NTS... BIT

I'm hungry.

Ich habe Hunger.

iSH H**ah**-B**uh** H**oo**N-G**ur**

I'm thirsty.

Ich habe Durst.

iSH H**ah**-B**uh** D**oo**RST

Is service included?

Ist das Trinkgeld inbegriffen?

iST D**ah**S TR**EE**NK-G**ê**LD

EEN-B**ê**-GR**EE**-F**ê**N

The bill, please.

Die Rechnung, bitte.

D**EE** R**ê**SH-N**ou**NG BIT

PHRASEMAKER

Ordering beverages is easy and a great way to practice your German! In many foreign countries you will have to request ice with your drinks.

Please bring me...

Bringen Sie mir...bitte

BR**EE**NG-**e**N Z**EE** M**EE**R... BIT

▶ **coffee...**

einen Kaffee

I-N**e**N K**ah**-F**A**

▶ **tea...**

einen Tee

I-N**e**N T**A**

▶ **with cream**

mit Sahne

M**I**T Z**ah**-N**uh**

▶ **with sugar**

mit Zucker

M**I**T TS**ou**-K**ur**

▶ **with lemon**

mit Zitrone

M**I**T TS**I**-TR**O**-N**uh**

▶ **with ice**

mit Eis

M**I**T **I**S

Soft drinks (alcohol free)

Alkoholfreies Getränk

@L-KO-H@L-FRD-@S G@-TR@NK

Milk

Milch

MOL^SH

Hot chocolate

heiße Schokolade

HD-S@ SHO-KO-L@-D@

Juice

Saft

Z@FT

Orange juice

Orangensaft

O-R@N-J@N-Z@FT

Ice water

Eiswasser

DS-V@-S@r

Mineral water

Mineralwasser

MO-N@-R@L-V@-S@r

AT THE BAR

Bartender

Barmixer

B@R-M@KS-@R

The wine list, please.

Die Weinliste, bitte.

D@ V@N-L@S-T@ BIT

Cocktail

einen Cocktail

@-N@N K@K-T@L

On the rocks

Auf Eis

@F @S

Straight

Ohne Eis

@-N@ @S

With lemon

Mit Zitrone

M@T TS@-TR@-N@

PHRASEMAKER

I would like a glass of...

Ich möchte ein Glas...

① ᴴ M⒰ⱼ ᴴ-T⒰ ①N GL⒜S...

▶ **champagne**

Sekt

Z⒠KT

▶ **beer**

Bier

B⒠R

▶ **wine**

Wein

V①N

▶ **red wine**

Rotwein

B⒪T-V①N

▶ **white wine**

Weißwein

V①S-V①N

ORDERING
BREAKFAST

In Germany breakfast is usually small, consisting of fresh rolls or warm bread with butter and honey accompanied by café au lait, hot tea, or hot chocolate.

Bread	**Toast**
Brot	Toast
BR⊙T	T⊙ST

---

with butter

mit Butter

M⊙T B⊚⎵-T⓾

---

with jam

mit Marmelade

M⊙T ⓂⓐⓇ-Ⓜⓔ-Lⓐ⎮D-⓾

Cereal

Sereal

S⊙-Rⓔⓔ-⓾L

Cereal

Müsli

M⊚⊚-SLⓔⓔ

PHRASEMAKER

I would like...

Ich möchte...

ᎣSH Mᴜ̈ʀˢᴴ-Tᴜʰ...

▶ **two eggs...**

zwei Eier...

TSVᎣ Ꭵ́-ᴜʀ...

▶ **scrambled eggs**   ▶ **fried eggs**

die Rühreier   die Spiegeleier

Dᴇᴇ Ʀᴏᴏ-ᴇ̈R-Ꭵ-ᴜʰ   Dᴇᴇ SH-Pᴇᴇ-Gᴇ̈L-Ꭵ-ᴜʀ

▶ **with bacon**

mit Speck

MᎣT SHPᴇ̈K

▶ **with ham**

mit Schinken

MᎣT SHᴇᴇNK-ᴇ̈N

▶ **with potatoes**

mit Kartoffeln

MᎣT KᴀʰR-TᎣF-ᴇ̈LN

LUNCH AND DINNER

Although you are encouraged to
sample great German cuisine, it is
important to be able to order foods
you are familiar with. This section will
provide words and phrases to help you.

I would like...

Ich möchte...

Ⓘ^{SH}　MⓊ'^{SH}-Tⓤ...

We would like...

Wir möchten...

Vⓔ R　MⓊ'^{SH}-Tⓔ N...

Please bring us...

Bringen Sie uns...bitte

BRⓔNG-Ⓔ N　Zⓔ　Ⓞ NS... BIT

The lady would like...

Die Dame möchte...

Dⓔ　Dⓐ'-Mⓤ　MⓊ'^{SH}-Tⓤ...

The gentleman would like...

Der Herr möchte...

Dⓔ R　Hⓔ R　MⓊ'^{SH}-Tⓤ...

STARTERS

Appetizers

Vorspeise

FOR-SHPI-Zuh

Bread and butter

Brot und Butter

BROT OUNT BOU-Tuh

Cheese

Käse

KA-Zuh

Fruit

Obst

OBST

Salad

Salat

Zah-Lah'T

Soup

Suppe

Zou-Puh

MEATS

Bacon
Speck
SHP@K

Beef
Rindfleisch
R@NT-FL@SH

Beef steak
Bifsteak
B@F-SHT@K

Ham
Schinken
SH@NK-@N

Lamb
Lamm
L@M

Pork
Schweinefleisch
SHV@-N@-FL@SH

Veal
Kalbfleisch
K@LP-FL@SH

POULTRY

Baked chicken

Backhuhn

B(ah)K-H(oo)N

Broiled chicken

Rosthuhn

R(O)ST-H(oo)N

Fried chicken

Brathuhn

BR(ah)T-H(oo)N

Duck

Ente

(ĕ)N-T(uh)

Goose

Gans

G(ah)NZ

Turkey

Truthahn

TR(oo)T-H(ah)N

SEAFOOD

Fish
Fisch
FⓘSH

Lobster
Hummer
Hⓞⓤ́-Mⓤⓡ

Oysters
Austern
ⓞⓦ́-STⓤⓡN

Salmon
Lachs
LⓐⓗKS

Shrimp
Krabben
KRⓐⓗ́-Bⓔ̃N

Trout
Forelle
FⓞR-ⓔ̃́-Lⓤⓗ

Tuna
Thunfisch
TⓞⓞN FⓘSH

OTHER ENTREES

Sandwich
Belegtes Brot

Bĕ-Lĕ́K-Tĕs BRⓄT

Hot dog (sausage)
Würstel

Vⓔⓦ́RS-Tĕ̄L

Hamburger
Hackfleisch

HⓐⓗK-FLⒶSH

French fries
Pommes Frites

PⓄ́-MĕS FRⒶTS

Pasta
Pasta

Pⓐⓗ́S-Tⓐⓗ

Pizza
Pizza

PⒺⒺ́T-Sⓐⓗ

VEGETABLES

Carrots

Karotten

K@ɦ-ʀO͞-TêN

Corn

Mais

MⒾS

Mushrooms

Pilze

PⒾL-TS⒰ɦ

Onions

Zwiebeln

TSVⒺ͞-BêLN

Potato

Kartoffeln

K@ɦR-TO͞F-êLN

Rice

Reis

ʀⒾS

Tomato

Tomaten

TⓄ-M@ɦ͞-TêN

FRUITS

Apple
Apfel
@P-F@L

Banana
Banane
B@-N@-N@

Grapes
Trauben
TR@-B@N

Lemon
Zitrone
TS@-TR@-N@

Orange
Orange
@-R@N-J@

Strawberry
Erdbeeren
@RT-B@R-@N

Watermelon
Wassermelone
V@-S@-M@-L@-N@

DESSERT

Dessert
Nachtisch
N(ah)K-T(i)SH

Apple pie
Apfeltorte
(ah)P-F(e)L-T(OR)R-T(uh)

Cherry pie
Kirschtorte
K(EE)RSH-T(OR)R-T(uh)

Pastries
Backwaren
B(ah)K-V(ah)R-(e)N

Candy
Konfekt
K(O)N-F(e)KT

Candy
Süssigkeiten
Z(ew)-S(i)SH-K(I)-T(e)N

Ice cream
Speiseeis
SHP**Ī**-Z**uh**-**Ī**S

Ice-cream cone
Eistüte
ĪS-T**ew**-T**uh**

Chocolate
Schokolade
SH**O**-K**O**-L**ah**-D**uh**

Strawberry
Erdbeeren
ĕRT-B**ĕ**R-**ĕ**N

Vanilla
Vanille
V**ah**-N**EE**-L**uh**

CONDIMENTS

Butter
Butter
B⓪⓪́-T⓪

Ketchup
Ketchup
Kⓔ́TCH-⓪P

Mayonnaise
Mayonnaise
M①-⓪-N④́-Z⓪

Mustard
Senf
ZⓔNF

Salt	**Pepper**
Salz	Pfeffer
Z④LTS	Pⓔ́-Pⓤ

Sugar
Zucker
TS⓪́K-ⓤ

Vinegar and oil
Essig und öl
ⓔ́-S①SH   ⓪NT   ⓤL

SETTINGS

A cup
Eine Tasse
Ī´-Nuh Tah´-Suh

A glass
Ein Glas
ĪN GLahS

A spoon
Ein Löffel
ĪN LUr´-FēL

A fork
Eine Gabel
Ī´-Nuh Gah´-BēL

A knife
Ein Messer
ĪN Mē´-SUr

A plate
Ein Teller
ĪN Tē´-LUr

A napkin
Eine Serviette
Ī´-Nuh Sē´R-Vēē-ē-´Tuh

HOW DO YOU WANT IT COOKED?

Baked
Gebacken
G**ẽ**-B**aⁿ**-K**ẽ**N

Broiled / Toasted
Gegrillt
G**ẽ**-GR**ö**LT

Steamed
Gedünstet
G**ẽ**-D**ou**NS-T**ẽ**T

Fried
Gebraten
G**ẽ**-BR**aⁿ**-T**ẽ**N

Rare
Leicht angebraten
L**i**SHT **aⁿ**N-G**ẽ**-BR**aⁿ**-T**ẽ**N

Medium
Halbdurch
H**aⁿ**LP D**oy**CH

Well done
Durchgebraten
D**oy**-**i**SH-G**ẽ**-BR**aⁿ**-T**ẽ**N

PROBLEMS

I didn't order this.

Ich habe das nicht bestellt..

①ᴴ H@ⁿ-B@ D@S N①ᴴT Bⓔ-SHTⓔ́LT

Is the bill correct?

Stimmt die Rechnung?

ST①MT Dⓔ Rⓔ́ᴴ-N@NG

Bring me...

Bringen Sie mir...

BRⓔ́NG-ⓔN Zⓔ MⓔR... BIT

GETTING AROUND

Getting around in a foreign country can be an adventure in itself! Taxi and bus drivers do not always speak English, so it is essential to be able to give simple directions. The words and phrases in this chapter will help you get where you're going.

- Negotiate the fare with your taxi driver in advance. The tip is usually included in the fare.

- Trains are used frequently by visitors to Europe. Schedules and timetables are easily understood. Arrive early to allow time for ticket purchasing and checking in, and remember, trains leave on time!

- **U-BAHN,** or the subway, is an inexpensive underground train system identified by a white "**U**" sign on a blue background.

- Check with your travel agent about special rail passes which allow unlimited travel within a set period of time.

KEY WORDS

Airport
Flughafen
FL00́K-H@h-F®N

Bus Station / Bus Stop
Bus Station
Bushaltestelle
B00S SHT@h́T-S®-0N
B00S-H@h́L-T@h-SHT®-L@h

Car Rental Agency
Auto Verleih
@ẃ-T0 F®́R-L0

Subway Station
U-Bahn Station
00́-B@hN SHT@h́T-S®-0N

Taxi Stand
Taxistand
T@hK-S®-SHT@hNT

Train Station
Bahnhof
B@h́N-H0F

AIR TRAVEL

Arrivals	**Departures**
Ankunft	Abfahrt
ⓐ́N-Kⓞ́NFT	ⓐ́P-Fⓐ́RT

Flight number...

Flugnummer...

FLⓞⓞK-Nⓞⓞ́-Mⓤᵣ...

Airline

Flugesellschaft

FLⓞⓞK-Gⓔ̃-Zⓔ̃́L-SHⓐFT

Gate

Ausgang

ⓞⱲ́S-Gⓐ́NG

Information

Auskunft

ⓞⱲ́S-KⓞⓤNFT

Ticket (airline)

Flugticket

FLⓞⓞK-Tⓘ-Kⓔ̃́T

Reservations

Reservierung

Rⓔ̃́-Zⓔ̃R-Vⓔⓔ́B-ⓞⓤNG

PHRASEMAKER

I would like a seat...

Ich möchte einen Platz...

ⒾSH MⓊrSH-Tⓤh Ⓘ-NⒺN PLⒶTS...

▶ **in first class**

in erster Klasse

ⒾN ⒺR-STⓊr KLⒶ-Sⓤh

▶ **in the no smoking section**

im Nichtraucher

ⒾM NⒾSH-TRⓄⓌ-KⓊr

▶ **next to the window**

am Fenster

ⒶM FⒺN-SHTⓊr

▶ **on the aisle**

am Gang

ⒶM GⒶNG

▶ **near the exit**

neben dem Ausgang

NⒶ-BⒺN DⒺM ⓄⓌS-GⒶNG

THE BUS

Bus

Bus

B⩲S

Where is the bus stop?

Wo ist die Bushaltestelle?

V⊙ ⓘST Dⓔⓔ B⩲S-Hⓐ⸍L-Tⓤⓗ-SHTⓔ⸍-Lⓤⓗ

Do you go to...?

Gehen Sie nach...?

Gⓐ⸍-ⓔN Zⓔⓔ NⓐⓗK...

What is the fare?

Wieviel ist die Karte?

Vⓔⓔ-FⓔⓔL ⓘST Dⓔⓔ KⓐⓗR-Tⓤⓗ

Do I need exact change?

Brauche ich genaues Kleingeld?

BRⓞⓦ⸍-Kⓤⓗ ⓘSH Gⓔ-Nⓞⓦ⸍-ⓔS

KLⓘⓝN-GⓔⓛD

How often do the buses run?

Wie oft gehen die Busse?

Vⓔⓔ ⓐⓗFT Gⓐ⸍-ⓔN Dⓔⓔ B⩲⸍-Sⓤⓗ

PHRASEMAKER

Please tell me...

Sagen Sie mir bitte...

ZAH'-GEN ZEE MEER BIT'-Tuh...

▸ **which bus goes to...**

welcher Bus geht nach...

VEL-SHUr BOUS GAT NAHK...

▸ **what time the bus leaves**

um wieviel Uhr fährt der Bus

OOM VEE'-FEEL OOR FERT DER BOUS

▸ **where the bus stop is**

wo ist die Bushaltestelle?

VO IST DEE BOUS-HAHL'-Tuh-SHTE'-Luh

▸ **where to get off**

wo ich aussteigen muß

VO ISH OW'S-SHTI-GEN MOUS

BY CAR

Fill it up.

Volltanken.

VⓄL-TⓐNK-ⓔN

Can you help me?

Können Sie mir helfen?

KⓊʼ-NⓔN ZⒺ MⒺR HⒺʼL-FⓔN

My car won't start.

Mein Auto startet nicht.

MⒾN ⓄWʼ-TⓄ SHTⓐʼR-TⓔT NⒾ^{SH}T

Can you fix it?

Können Sie den Wagen reparieren ?

KⓊʼ-NⓔN ZⒺ DⓔN Vⓐʼ-GⓐN

Rⓔʼ-PⓐⓇ-ⒺʼR-ⓔN

What will it cost?

Wieviel kostet es?

VⒺʼ-FⒺL KⓄʼS-TⓔT ⓔS

How long will it take?

Wie lange brauchen Sie?

VⒺ LⓐʼN-GⓊⓗ BRⓄWʼ-KⓔN ZⒺ

PHRASEMAKER

Please check...

Prüfen Sie...bitte

PRew-FeN ZEE... BIT

▶ **the battery**

die Batterie

DEE Bah-Tuh-REE

▶ **the brakes**

die Bremsen

DEE BReM-ZeN

▶ **the oil**

das Öl

DahS UrL

▶ **the tires**

die Reifen

DEE RI-FeN

▶ **the water**

das Wasser

DahS Vah-SUr

SUBWAYS AND TRAINS

Where is the subway station?

Wo ist die U-Bahn?

V◎ ①ST D㋹ ◎◎́-B㋐N

Where is the train station?

Wo ist der Bahnhof?

V◎ ①ST D㋕R B㋐N-H◎F

A one-way ticket, please.

Einzel Karte, bitte.

①N-TS㋋L K㋐R-T㋒ BIT

A round trip ticket.

Hin und zurück.

H①N ㋒NT TS◎◎́-B㋛K

First class

Erste Klasse

㋋R-ST㋒ KL㋐́-S㋒

Second class

Zweite Klasse

TSV①-T㋒ KL㋐́-S㋒

Which train do I take to go to...

Welchen Zug nehme ich nach...

VĕL-SHĕN TSOOK NÁ-Muh iSH Nahk...

What is the fare?

Wieviel ist die Karte?

VEE-FEEL iST DEE Kahr-Tuh

Is this seat taken?

Ist hier noch frei?

iST HEER NOK FRiI

Do I have to change trains?

Muß ich umsteigen?

MOOS iSH OOM-SHTi-GĕN

Does this train stop at...

Haltet der Zug in...?

Hahlt-ĕT DĕR TSOOK iN...

Where are we?

Wo sind wir?

VO ZiNT VEER

BY TAXI

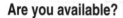

Can you call a taxi for me?

Können Sie mir ein Taxi rufen?

KÜr-NēN ZEE MēR ĪN
TahK-SEE ROO-FēN

Are you available?

Sind Sie frei?

ZĪNT ZEE FRĪ

I want to go...

Ich möchte zum...gehen.

ĪSH MÜSH-Tuh TSOOM...GĀ-ēN

Stop here, please.

Halten Sie hier, bitte.

HahL-TēN ZEE HēR BIT

Please wait.

Warten sie, bitte.

VahR-TēN ZEE BIT

How much do I owe?

Wieviel kostet es?

VEE-FēL KŌS-TēT ēS

PHRASEMAKER

I would like to go...

Ich möchte...

(i)^{SH} M(u)$^{'SH}$-T(uh)...

▸ **to this address**

zu dieser Adresse gehen

TS(oo) D(EE)-Z(ur) (ah)-DR(ë)-S(uh) G(A)-(ë)N

▸ **to the airport**

zum Flughafen gehen

TS(oo)M FL(oo)K-H(ah)-F(ë)N G(A)-(ë)N

▸ **to the bank**

zur Bank gehen

TS(oo)R B(ah)NK G(A)-(ë)N

▸ **to the hotel**

zum Hotel gehen

TS(oo)M H(O)-T(ë)L G(A)-(ë)N

▸ **to the hospital**

zum Krankenhaus gehen

TS(oo)M KR(ah)NK-(ë)N-H(ow)S G(A)-(ë)N

▸ **to the subway station**

zur U-Bahn gehen

TS(ur) (oo)-B(ah)N G(A)-(ë)N

SHOPPING

Whether you plan a major shopping spree or just need to purchase some basic necessities, the following information is useful.

- Shops are usually open between 9 AM and 6 PM, closing 2 to 3 hours in the afternoon.

- On Saturday most shops close around 1 PM.

- You are likely to encounter an item called VAT, (value-added tax) on purchases. Fortunately, many countries return this tax upon departure. In some instances you may receive a discount in the shop.

- Always keep receipts for everything you buy! This will be helpful in filling out the customs declaration when you return home.

SIGNS TO LOOK FOR:

BUCHHANDLUNG (Bookstore)

SUPERMARKT (Supermarket)

WARENHAUS (Department store)

KEY WORDS

Credit card

Kreditkarte

KR(ē)-D(ÉÉ)T-K(ah)R-T(uh)

Money

Geld

G(ē)LT

Receipt

Quittung

KV(ī)-T(ou)NG

Sale

Sonder preis

Z(Ó)N-D(ur) PR(Ī)S

Store

Laden

L(ah)-D(ē)N

Traveler's checks

Reiseschecks

R(Ī)-Z(uh)-SH(ē)KS

USEFUL PHRASES

Do you sell...?

Verkaufen Sie...?

F(ĕ)R-K(ow)́-F(ĕ)N Z(EE)...

Do you have...?

Haben Sie...

H(ah)́-B(ĕ)N Z(EE)...

I want to buy...

Ich möchte kaufen...

(i)SH M(Ur)́SH-T(uh) K(ow)́-F(ĕ)N...

How much?

Wieviel?

V(EE)́-F(EE)L

No thank you.

Nein, danke.

N(I)N D(ah)́N-K(uh)

I´m just looking.

Ich schaue mich nur um.

(i)SH SH(ow)́-(uh) M(i)SH N(oo)R (ou)M

It's very expensive

Es ist sehr teuer

ĔS ĬST SĔR TOY-Ur

Can't you give me a discount?

Können Sie mir einen Preisnachlass geben?

KUr-NĕN ZEE MĔR Ĭ-NĕN

PRĬS-NahK-LahS GĀ-BĕN

I'll take it!

Ich nehme es!

ĬSH NĀ-Muh ĔS

I'd like a receipt, please.

Ich möchte eine Quittung, bitte.

ĬSH MUrSH-Tuh Ĭ-Nuh

KVĬ-TooNG BIT

I want to return this.

Ich möchte das zurück bringen.

ĬSH MUrSH-Tuh DahS TSoo-RooK

BRĔNG-ĕN

PHRASEMAKER

I'm looking for...

Ich suche ...

Ⓘ⁻ˢᴴ Zⓞⓞ⁻Ⓚⓤⓗ...

▶ **a bakery**

eine Bäckerei

Ⓘ⁻Nⓤⓗ Bⓔ̈⁻Ⓚⓤⓗ⁻Rⓘ

▶ **a bank**

eine Bank

Ⓘ⁻Nⓤⓗ Bⓐ̈NK

▶ **a bookstore**

einen Buch laden

Ⓘ⁻Nⓔ̈N BⓞⓞK Lⓐⓗ⁻Dⓔ̈N

▶ **a hair salon**

den Friseursalon

Dⓔ̈N FRⓔⓔ⁻ZⓞⓞR⁻Sⓐⓗ⁻Lⓐⓗ́N

▶ **a pharmacy**

die Apotheke

Dⓔⓔ ⓐⓗ⁻PO⁻TⒶ⁻Ⓚⓤⓗ

▶ **a photo shop**

einen Fotoladen

Ⓘ⁻Nⓔ̈N FO⁻TO⁻Lⓐⓗ⁻Dⓔ̈N

PHRASEMAKER

Do you sell...

Verkaufen Sie...?

FⓔR-Kⓞⓦ-FⓔN ZⒺ...

▸ **aspirin?**

Aspirin?

ⓐ-SPⒺ-RⒺN

▸ **cigarettes?**

Zigaretten?

TSⒺ-Gⓐ-Rⓔ-TⓔN

▸ **deodorant?**

Deo?

DⒶ-Ⓞ

▸ **dresses?**

Kleider?

KLⒾ-DⓊr

▸ **film?**

Film?

FⒾLM

▶ **pantyhose?**

Strümpfe?

SHTR@PH-F@

▶ **perfume?**

Parfüm?

P@R-F@M

▶ **razor blades?**

Rasierklingen?

R@-Z@R-KL@N-G@

▶ **shampoo?**

Shampoo?

SH@M-P@

▶ **shaving cream?**

Rasiercreme?

R@-Z@R-KR@-M@

▶ **soap?**

Seife?

Z@-F@

▶ **shirts?**

Hemden?

H@M-D@N

▸ **sunglasses?**

Sonnenbrille?

ZŌ-NĒN-BRȮ-Lᵘʰ

▸ **sunscreen?**

Sonnenschutzcreme?

ZŌ-NĒN-SHᵒᵘTS-KRȂ-Mᵘʰ

▸ **toothbrushes?**

Zahnbürste?

TSȃʰN-BᵉʷRS-Tᵘʰ

▸ **toothpaste?**

Zahnpaste?

TSȃʰN-PȃʰS-Tᵘʰ

▸ **water?** (bottled)

eine Flasche Wasser

Ȋ-Nᵘʰ FLȃʰ-SHᵘʰ Vȃʰ-SᵁʳR

▸ **water?** (mineral)

Mineralwasser

MȊ-NĒ-RȃʰL-Vȃʰ-SᵁʳR

ESSENTIAL SERVICES

THE BANK

As a traveler in a foreign country your primary contact with banks will be to exchange money.

- Have your passport handy when changing money.

- Change enough funds before leaving home to pay for tips, food, and transportation to your final destination.

- Generally, you will receive a better rate of exchange at a bank, but rates can change from bank to bank.

- The euro is the new "single currency" of the European Monetary Union, and Germany is a participating nation.

- Cash is the accepted form of payment in Germany; however, ATMs accept a wide variety of credit cards.

KEY WORDS

Bank

Die Bank

DEE BahNK

Exchange office

Wechselstube

VEK-SEL-SHToo-Buh

Money

Geld

GELT

Money order

Die Postanweisung

DEE POST-ahN-VI-ZooNG

Traveler's checks

Reiseschecks

RI-Zuh-SHEKS

USEFUL PHRASES

Where is the bank?

Wo ist die Bank?

V⊚ ⓘST D€€ B⒜NK

What time does the bank open?

Wann macht die Bank auf?

V⒜N M⒜KT D€€ B⒜NK ⓞⓦF

Where is the exchange office?

Wo ist die Wechselstube?

V⊚ ⓘST D€€ V⒠K-S⒠L-SHT⓪⓪-B⒰

What time does the exchange office open?

Wann macht die Wechselstube auf?

V⒜N M⒜KT D€€
V⒠K-S⒠L-SHT⓪⓪-B⒰ ⓞⓦF

Can I change dollars here?

Kann ich hier Geld wechseln?

K⒜N ⓘ^{SH} H€€R G⒠LT V⒠K-S⒠LN

Can you change this?

Können Sie das wechseln?

KÜr-NĕN ZĒĒ DahS VĕK-SĕLN

What is the exchange rate?

Was ist der Kurs für heute?

VahS iST DĕR KooRS
FewR Hoy-Tuh

I would like large bills.

Ich möchte große Geldscheine.

iSH MÜrSH-Tuh GROO-Suh
GĕLT-SHi-Nuh

I would like small bills.

Ich möchte kleine Geldscheine.

iSH MÜrSH-Tuh KLi-Nuh
GĕLT-SHi-Nuh

I need change.

Ich brauche Kleinegeld.

iSH BRow-Kuh KLi-N-GĕLT

Do you have an ATM?

Haben Sie einen Geldautomat?

Hah-BĕN ZĒĒ i-NĕN
GĕLT-ow-TO-MahT

POST OFFICE

If you plan to send letters and postcards, be sure to send them early so that you don't arrive home before they do. **POSTAMT** identifies the post office.

KEY WORDS

Airmail

Luftpost

L(ou)FT-P(O)ST

Letter

Brief

BR(EE)F

Post office

Postamt

P(O)ST-(ah)MT

Postcard

Postkarte

P(O)ST-K(ah)R-T(uh)

Stamps

Briefmarken

(I)-N(uh) BR(EE)F-M(ah)R-K(ĕ)N

USEFUL PHRASES

Where is the post office?

Wo ist das Postamt?

VO OST DahS POST-ahMT

What time does the post office open?

Wann macht die Post auf?

VahN MahKT DEE POST OWF

I need stamps.

Ich brauche Briefmarken.

OSH BRow-Kuh BREEF-MahR-KeN

I need an envelope.

Ich brauche einen Umschlag.

OSH BRow-Kuh O-NeN ouM-SHLahK

I need a pen.

Ich brauche einen Kugelschreiber.

OSH BRow-Kuh O-NeN
Koo-GeL-SHReO-BeR

TELEPHONE

Placing phone calls in a foreign
country can be a test of will and
stamina! Besides the obvious
language barriers, service can vary greatly from
one town to the next.

- In Germany, phone calls can be made from
  the post office.

- Public pay phones have multilingual in-
  structions on how to use them.

- Making calls from your hotel can add hefty
  service charges to your bill.

KEY WORDS

Information
Auskunft
@S-K@NFT

Long distance
Ferngespräch
F@RN-G@-SHPR@SH

Operator
Telefonist
T@-L@-F@N-@ST

Phone book
Telefonbuch
T@-L@-F@N-B@K

Public telephone
öffentliches Telefon
@-F@NT-L@-SH@S T@-L@-F@N

Telephone
Telefon
T@-L@-F@N

USEFUL PHRASES

May I use your telephone?

Darf ich bitte telefonieren?

D@RF ①ˢᴴ B①́-T⓾

T⑥́-L⑥-F⓪-N⑧R-⑥N

I don't speak German.

Ich spreche kein Deutsch.

①ˢᴴ SHPR⑥́ˢᴴ⓾ K①N D⓪TCH

I would like to make a long-distance call.

Ich möchte ein Ferngespräch machen.

①ˢᴴ M⓾́ˢᴴ-T⓾ ①N

F@RN-G⑥-SHPR⑥K M@K-⑥N

I would like to make a call to the United States.

Ich möchte die U.S.A. anrufen.

①ˢᴴ M⓾́ˢᴴ-T⓾ D⑧ ⓪⓪ ⑥S @

@N-R⓪⓪́-F⑥N

I want to call this number...

Ich möchte Nummer...

Ⓘ^SH MⓊr'^SH-Tⓤh Nⓞⓞ-MⓊr...

1 eins ⒾNS	**2** zwei TSVⓀ	**3** drei DR~Ⓘ
4 vier FⒺⒺR	**5** fünf FⒺⓌNF	**6** sechs ZⒺ̃KS
7 sieben ZⒺⒺ-BⒺ̃N	**8** acht ⒶⓗKT	**9** neun NⓄⓎN
✳	**0** null NⓄⓊL	**#**

SIGHTSEEING AND ENTERTAINMENT

In most towns in Germany you will find tourist information offices. Here you can usually obtain brochures, maps, historical information, bus and train schedules.

CITIES IN GERMANY

Berlin
B⒰r-L⒤N

Frankfurt
FR⒜NK-F⒰T

Munich
M⒠ⓦ-N⒤K

Stuttgart
SHT⒪⒰T-G⒜hRT

Hamburg
H⒜hM-B⒰rG

KEY WORDS

Admission

Eintritt

ĺN-TRⓘT

Map

Landkarte

LⓐʰNT-KⓐʰR-Tⓤʰ

Reservation

Reservierung

Rⓔ̃-Zⓔ̃R-VⓔⓔR-ⓞⓤNG

Ticket

Ticket

Tⓘʹ-Kⓔ̃T

Tour

Tour

TⓞⓞR

Tour guide

Reiseleiter

Rⓘʹ-Zⓤʰ-Lⓘ-Tⓤʳ

USEFUL PHRASES

Where is the tourist office?

Wo ist das Reisebüro?

VO ⒤ST D@S
RⒾ-Z⒰-B⒠ⓦ-RO

Is there a tour to...?

Gibt es eine Tour nach...?

G⒠PT ⒠S Ⓘ-N⒰ TⓄⓄR N@K

Where do I buy a ticket?

Wo kann ich eine Karte kaufen?

VO K@N Ⓘ^SH Ⓘ-N⒰ K@R-T⒰
K⒪ⓦ-F⒠N

How much does the tour cost?

Wieviel kostet die Reise-tour?

V⒠⒠-F⒠⒠L KⓄS-T⒠T
D⒠⒠ RⒾ-Z⒰ TⓄⓄR

How long does the tour take?

Wie lange dauert die Rundfahrt?

V⒠⒠ L@N-G⒰ D⒪ⓦ-ⓊRT D⒠⒠
R⒪ⓤNT-F@RT

Does the guide speak English?

Spricht der Reiseführer Englisch?

SPRⓘSHT DⓔR RⒾ-Zⓤ-Fⓔw-RⓊr ⒺN-GLⓘSH

Are children free?

Sind die Kinder umsonst?

ZⓘNT DⒺ KⓘN-DⓊr ⓄⓌM-ZⓄNST

What time does the show start?

Wann fängt die Ausstellung an?

VⒶN FⒺNGT DⒺ ⓄⓌS-SHTⓤ-LⓄⓌNG ⒶN

Do I need reservations?

Brauche ich Reservierung?

BRⓄⓌ-Kⓤ ⓘSH Rⓔ-ZⒺR-VⒺR-ⓄⓌNG

Where can we go dancing?

Wo können wir tanzen gehen?

WⓄ KⓊr-NⒺN VⒺR TⒶN-TSⒺN GⒶ-ⒺN

Is there a cover charge?

Kostet es Eintritt?

KⒶS-TⒺT ⒺS ⓘN-TRⓘT

PHRASEMAKER

May I invite you...

Darf ich Sie...

D@RF ①ˢᴴ Z①...

▶ **to a concert?**

ins Konzert einladen?

①NTS K@́N-TS①RT ①́N-L@h-D①N

▶ **to dance?**

zum Tanzen einladen?

TS⑩M T@́N-TS①N ①́N-L@h-D①N

▶ **to dinner?**

zum Abendessen einladen?

TS⑩M @h́-B①NT-①S-①N
①́N-L@h-D①N

▶ **to the movies?**

ins Kino einladen?

①NTS K①́-N⑩ ①́N-L@h-D①N

▶ **to the theater?**

ins Theater einladen?

①NS T①-@h́-T⑪r ①́N-L@h-D①N

PHRASEMAKER

Where can I find...

Wo findet man...

VŌ FĬN-DĔT MⓐN...

▶ **a health club?**

ein Fitnesstudio?

ⒾN FĬT-NĔS SHTⓞⓞ-DⒺⒺ-Ⓞ

▶ **a swimming pool?**

ein Schwimmbad?

ⒾN SHVⒾM-BⓐT

▶ **a tennis court?**

einen Tennisplatz?

Ⓘ-NĔN TĔ-NⒾS-PLⓐTS

▶ **a golf course?**

einen Golfplatz?

Ⓘ-NĔN GŌLF-PLⓐTS

HEALTH

Hopefully you will not need medical attention on your trip. If you do, it is important to communicate basic information regarding your condition. Here are some helpful tips to help you in this situation.

- Check with your insurance company before leaving home to find out if you are covered in a foreign country.

- Have your prescriptions translated before you leave home.

- Take a small first-aid kit with you.

- Your embassy or consulate should be able to assist you in finding health care.

KEY WORDS

Ambulance

Krankenwagen

KRⓐ̇NK-ⓔN-Vⓐ-Gⓔ̲N

Dentist

Zahnarzt

TSⓐ̇N-ⓐRTST

Doctor

Arzt

ⓐRTST

Emergency!

Ein Notfall!

ⒾN NⓄ́T-Fⓐ̇L

Hospital

Krankenhaus

KRⓐ̇NK-ⓔ̲N-Hⓞ̇wS

Prescription

Rezept

Rⓔ̈TS-ⓔ́PT

USEFUL PHRASES

I am sick.

Ich bin krank.

Ⓘˢᴴ BⒾN KRⓐⒽNK

I need a doctor.

Ich brauche einen Arzt.

Ⓘˢᴴ BRⓄⱲ-Ⓚⓤⱨ Ⓘ-NⒺN ⓐⱨRTST

It's an emergency!

Es ist ein Notfall!

ⒺS ⒾST ⒾN NⓄT-FⓐⱨL

Where is the nearest hospital?

Wo ist ein Krankenhaus in der Nähe?

VⓄ ⒾST ⒾN KRⓐⱨNK-ⒺN-HⓄⱲS
ⒾN DⒺR Nⓐ-ⓤⱨ

Call an ambulance!

Rufen Sie einen Krankenwagen!

RⓄⓄ-FⒺN ZⒺⒺ Ⓘ-NⒺN
KRⓐⱨNK-ⒺN-Vⓐⱨ-GⒺN

I'm allergic to...

Ich bin allergisch gegen...

Ⓘˢᴴ BⒾN ⓐⱨ-LⒺ̆R-GⒾˢᴴ GⒶ́-GⒺ̱N...

I'm pregnant.

Ich bin schwanger.

Ⓘˢᴴ BⒾN SHVⓐⱨN-GⓊⱱ

I'm diabetic.

Ich bin zuckerkrank.

Ⓘˢᴴ BⒾN TSⓄⓤ́-KⓊⱱ-KBⓐⱨNK

I have a heart condition.

Ich bin herzkrank.

Ⓘˢᴴ BⒾN HⒺ̆RTS-KBⓐⱨNK

I have high blood pressure.

Ich habe hohen Blutdruck.

Ⓘˢᴴ Hⓐⱨ́-Bⓤⱨ HⓄ́-Ⓔ̱N BLⓄⓄT-Bⓞⓤ́K

I have low blood pressure.

Ich habe niedrigen Blutdruck.

Ⓘˢᴴ Hⓐⱨ́-Bⓤⱨ NⒺⒺ́-DBⒺⒺ-Gⓔ̱N
BLⓄⓄT-Bⓞⓤ́K

PHRASEMAKER

I need...

Ich brauche...

▸ **a doctor**

einen Arzt

▸ **a dentist**

einen Zahnarzt

Ⓘ-NⒺN TSⓐN-ⓐRTST

▸ **a nurse**

eine Krankenschwester

▸ **an optician**

einen Optiker

Ⓘ-NⒺN Ⓞ-PⒾ-Kⓤⓗ

▸ **a pharmacist**

einen Apotheker

Ⓘ-NⒺN ⓐ-PⓄ-TⒶ-Kⓤⓗ

PHRASEMAKER
AT THE PHARMACY

Do you have...?

Haben Sie...

H@h-B@N Z@...

▶ **aspirin?**

Aspirin?

@h-SP@-R@N

▶ **Band-Aids?**

Pflaster?

FL@h-ST@r

▶ **cough medicine?**

Hustenmittel

H@@S-T@N M@-T@L

▶ **ear drops?**

Ohrentropfen?

@-R@N-TR@P-F@N

▶ **eyedrops?**

Augentropfen?

@w-G@N-TR@P-F@N

BUSINESS TRAVEL

It is important to show appreciation and interest in another person's language and culture, particularly when doing business. A few well-pronounced phrases can make a great impression.

I have an appointment.

Ich habe einen Termin.

①ᔆᴴ Hah-Buh ①-N℮N T℮R-M℮℮N

Here is my card.

Hier ist meine Visitenkarte.

H℮℮R ①ST M①-Nuh V℮℮-Z℮℮-T℮N-Kah-R-Tuh

I need an interpreter?

Ich brauche einen Übersetzer?

①ᔆᴴ BRow-Kuh ①-N℮N ℮w-B℮R-Z℮T-Sur

May I speak to Mr...?

Darf ich bitte Herrn...sprechen?

Dah-RF ①ᔆᴴ B①-Tuh H℮RN... SHPR℮-ᔆᴴ℮N

May I speak to Mrs...?

Darf ich bitte Frau...sprechen...?

Dah-RF ①ᔆᴴ B①-Tuh FRow...SHPR℮-ᔆᴴ℮N_

KEY WORDS

Appointment

Termin

TĕR-MĒN

Meeting

Konferenz

Kahn-Fĕ-RĕNTS

Marketing

Marketing

MahR-Kĕ-TEEN

Presentation

Präsentation

PRĀ-SĕN-Tah-TSEE-ON

Sales

Verkauf

FĕR-Kowf

PHRASEMAKER

I need...

Ich brauche...

(i)SH BR(ow)-K(uh)...

▸ **a computer**

einen Computer

(I)-N(ĕ)N K(o)M-P(ew)-T(ur)

▸ **a copy machine**

eine Kopiermaschine

(I)-N(uh) K(o)-P(ee)-(ur) M(uh)-SH(ee)-N(uh)

▸ **a conference room**

einen Konferenzraum

(I)-N(ĕ)N K(ah)N-F(ĕ)-R(ĕ)NTS-R(ah)M

▸ **a fax machine**

eine Faxmaschine

(I)-N(uh) F(ah)KS-M(ah)-SH(ee)-N(uh)

▸ **an interpreter**

einen Übersetzer

(I)-N(ĕ)N (ew)-B(ur)-Z(ĕ)T-S(ur)

▸ **a lawyer**

der Rechtsanwalt

DⒺR RⒺᶜᴴTS-ⓐN-VⓐLT

▸ **a notary**

einen Notar

Ⓘ-NⒺN NⓄ-TⓐR

▸ **overnight delivery**

übernacht Zustellung

ⓔⱳ-BⓤrR-NⓤᴴKT TSⓄⓄ-SHTⒺL-ⓔⱳNG

▸ **paper**

Papier

Pⓐ-PⒺⒺR

▸ **a ballpoint pen**

einen Kuli

Ⓘ-NⒺN KⓄⓄ-LⒺⒺ

▸ **a pencil**

einen Bleistift

Ⓘ-NⒺN BLⒾ-SHTⒾFT

▸ **a secretary**

einen Sekretärin

Ⓘ-NⒺN SⒺK-RⒺ-TⒺR-ⒾN

GENERAL INFORMATION

Germany enjoys a temperate climate. Germanys sights, sounds, and charm have something to offer everyone!

SEASONS

Spring

der Frühling

DⓔR FRⓔW-LⓔⓔNG

Summer

der Sommer

DⓔR ZŌ-MⓊr

Winter

der Winter

DⓔR VⓘN-TⓊr

Autumn

der Herbst

DⓔR HⓔRPST

THE DAYS

Monday
Montag
MÓN-T@hG

Tuesday
Dienstag
DÉENS-T@hG

Wednesday
Mittwoch
MÓT-VOK

Thursday
Donnerstag
DÓ-NUr-ST@hG

Friday
Freitag
FRÍ-T@hG

Saturday
Samstag
Z@hMS-T@hG

Sunday
Sonntag
ZÓN-T@hG

THE MONTHS

January
Januar
Yah-Noo-ahR

February
Februar
FA-BRoo-ahR

March
März
MÖRTS

April
April
ah-PREEL

May
Mai
MI

June
Juni
Yoo-NEE

July
Juli
Yoo-LEE

August
August
ow-GooST

September
September
ZÖP-TÖM-BUrR

October
Oktober
OK-TO-BUr

November
November
NO-VÖM-BUr

December
Dezember
DA-TSÖM-BUr

COLORS

Black	**White**
Schwarz	Weiß
SHV@RTS	V①S
Blue	**Brown**
Blau	Braun
BL@	BR@N
Gray	**Gold**
Grau	Gold
GR@	G@LD
Orange	**Yellow**
Orange	Gelb
①-R@N-J@	G@LP
Red	**Green**
Rot	Grün
R①T	GR@N
Pink	**Purple**
Rosa	Lila
R①-Z@	L@-L@

NUMBERS

0	1	2
Null	eins	zwei
N⊚L	①NS	TSV①

3	4	5
drei	vier	fünf
DR①	F⊕R	F⊚NF

6	7	8
sechs	sieben	acht
Z⊕KS	Z⊕-B⊕N	ⓐ⊠T

9	10	11
neun	zehn	elf
N⊚N	TS⊛N	ⓔLF

12	13	14
zwölf	dreizehn	vierzehn
TSV⊚LF	DR①-TS⊛N	F⊕R-TS⊛N

15	16	17
fünfzehn	sechzehn	siebzehn
F⊚NF-TS⊛N	Z⊕K-TS⊛N	Z⊕P-TS⊛N

18	19	
achtzehn	neunzehn	
ⓐ⊠T-TS⊛N	N⊚N-TS⊛N	

20
zwanzig
TSV@N-TS①K

30
dreissig
DR①-S①K

40
vierzig
F€€R-TS①K

50
fünfzig
F@NF-TS①K

60
sechzig
Z€KS-TS①K

70
siebzig
Z€€B-TS①K

80
achtzig
@KT-TS①K

90
neunzig
N@N-TS①K

100
(ein) hundert
①N H@N-D€RT

1000
(ein) tausend
①N T@-Z€NT

1,000,000
eine Million
①-N@ M①L-Y①-N@

DICTIONARY

Each English entry is followed by the German word and then the EPLS Vowel Symbol System. Gender of nouns and adjectives is indicated by (m) for masculine and (f) for feminine where appropriate.

A

a, an ein / einer / eine ⓘN / ⓘ-Nⓤr / ⓘ-Nⓤh

a lot viel FⓔⓔL

able (to be) können Kⓤr-NⓔN

above über ⓔw-Bⓤr

accident der Unfall DⓔR ⓞⓞN-FⓐhL

accommodation die Unterkunft

　　Dⓔⓔ ⓞⓞN-Tⓤr-KⓤⓤNFT

account das Konto DⓐhS KⓞN-Tⓞ

address die Adresse Dⓔⓔ ⓐh-DRⓔ-Sⓤh

admission der Eintritt DⓔR ⓘN-TRⓘT

afraid Angst haben ⓐhNGST Hⓐh-BⓔN

after nachher NⓐhK-HⓔR

afternoon der Nachmittag DⓔR NⓐhK-Mⓘ-TⓐhG

agency das Büro DⓐhS Bⓔw-Bⓞ

air-conditioning die Klimaanlage

    DEE KLEE-Mah-ah-N-Lah-Guh

aircraft das Flugzeug DahS FLOOK-TSoyK

airline die Fluggesellschaft

    DEE FLOOK-Geh-Zel-SHahFT

airport der Flughafen DeR FLOOK-Hah-FeN

aisle am Gang ahM GahNG

aisle seat der Gangplatz DeR GahNG-PLahZ

all alle ah-Luh

almost fast FahST

alone allein ah-LIN

also auch owK

always immer I-MUr

ambulance der Krankenwagen

    DeR KRahNK-eN-VahG-eN

American der Amerikaner (m)

    DeR ah-Me-REE-Kah-NUr

    die Amerikanerin (f)

    DEE ah-Me-REE-Kah-NUr-IN

and und ouNT

another noch ein NOK IN

anything irgendwas EER-GeNT-VahS

apartment die Wohnung   DEE VO'-NooNG

appetizers die Vorspeise   DEE FO'R-SHPI-Zuh

apple der Apfel   DeR ah'P-FeL

appointment die Verabredung

    DEE FeR-ah'P-Rah-DooNG

April der April   DeR ah-PReEL

arrival die Ankunft   DEE ah'N-KooNFT

arrive (to) ankommen   ah'N-KO'-MeN

ashtray der Aschenbecher   DeR ah-SHeN-Be'-KUr

aspirin das Aspirin   DahS ah'S-PEE-ReEN

attention Achtung   ah'K-TooNG

August der August   DeR ow'-GooST

Australia Australia   owS-TRah-LEE-ah

    der Australier   DeR owS-TRah-LEE-Ur

    die Australierin   DEE owS-TRah-LEE-e-ReN

author der Autor   DeR ow-TO'R

automobile das Auto   DahS ow'-TO

Autumn der Herbst   DeR HeRPST

avenue die Strasse   DEE SHTRah'-Suh

awful schrecklich   SHReK'-LOSH

B

baby das Baby   DahS BA'-BEE

babysitter der Babysitter DⓔR BⒶ-BⒺⒺ-SⒾ-TⓊʳ

bacon der Speck DⓔR SHPⒺK

bad schlimm SHLⒾM

bag die Tasche DⒺⒺ TⒶʰ-SHⓊʰ

baggage das Gepäck DⒶʰS GⒺ-PⒺK

baked gebacken GⒶ-BⒶʰK-ⒺN

bakery die Bäckerei DⒺⒺ BⒺ-KⓊʰ-RⒾ

banana die Banane DⒺⒺ BⒶʰ-NⒶʰ-NⓊʰ

Band-Aid das Pflaster DⒶʰS FLⒶʰ-STⓔR

bank die Bank DⒺⒺ BⒶNK

barbershop der Herrenfriseur

   DⓔR HⒺʳB-ⒺN-FRⒺⒺ-ZⓊʳ

bartender der Barkeeper DⓔR BⒶʳB-KⒺⒺ-PⓊʳ

bath das Bad DⒶʰS BⒶʰD

bathing suit der Badeanzug DⓔR BⒶʰ-DⓊʰ-ⒶʰN-TSⓄⓄG

bathroom das Bad DⒶʰS BⒶʰD

battery die Batterie DⒺⒺ BⒶʰ-TⓊʰ-RⒺⒺ

beach der Strand DⓔR SHTRⒶʰNT

beautiful schön SHⓊN

beauty shop der Friseursalon

   DⓔR FRⒺⒺ-ZⓊʰR-SⒶʰ-LON

bed das Bett DⒶʰS BⒺT

beef das Rindfleisch   DahS   RINT-FLISH

beer das Bier   DahS   BEER

bellman der Hoteldiener   DeR   HO-TeL-DEE-NUr

belt der Gürtel   DeR   Gew-TeL

big groß   GROS

bill die Rechnung   DEE   ReSH-NOoNG

black schwarz   SHVahRTS

blanket die Decke   DEE   DeK-Kuh

blue blau   BLow

boat das Boot   DahS   BOT

book das Buch   DahS   BooK

bookstore der Buchladen   DeR   BooK-Lah-DeN

border die Grenze   DEE   GReN-TSuh

boy der Junge   DeR   YooNG-uh

bracelet das Armband   DahS   ahRM-BahNT

brake die Bremse   DEE   BReM-Zuh

bread das Brot   DahS   BROT

breakfast das Frühstück   DahS   FRew-SHTooK

broiled gegrillt   GeGRiLT

brown braun   BRowN

brush die Bürste   DEE   BewR-STuh

building das Gebäude   DahS   GeBoyDuh

bus der Bus DeR BouS

bus station die Station

    Dee BouS SHTah-TSee-ON

bus stop die Bushaltestelle

    Dee BouS-Hah'L-Tuh-SHTe-Luh

business das Geschäft DahS Ge-SHeFT

butter die Butter Dee Bou-TUr

buy (to) kaufen Kow-Fe̲N

C

cab das Taxi DahS Tah'K-See

call (to) rufen Roo-Fe̲N

camera der Fotoapparat

    DeR FO-TO-ah-Pah-RahT

Canada Kanada Kah-Nah-Dah

    der Kanadier DeR Kah-Nah-Dee-Ur

    der Kanadierin Dee Kah-Nah-Dee-e-ReN

candy das Konfekt DahS KON-FeKT

car das Auto DahS ow-TO

carrot die Karotte Dee Kah-RO-Tuh

castle das Schloss DahS SHLOS

cathedral der Dom DeR DOM

celebration das Fest DahS FeST

center das Zentrum DⓐS TSⒺN-TRⓄM

chair der Stuhl DⒺR SHTⓄⓄL

champagne der Sekt DⒺR SⒺKT

change (to) wechseln VⒺK-SⒺLN

change (exact) Kleingeld KLⒶN-GⒺLD

cheap billig BⒾ-LⒾK

check (restaurant bill) die Rechnung

     DⒺ RⒺSH-NⓄNG

cheers! Prost PBⓄST

cheese der Käse DⒺR KⒶ-Sⓤⓗ

chicken das Huhn DⓐS HⓄⓄN

child das Kind DⓐS KⒾNT

chocolate (flavor) Schokolade SHⓄ-KⓄ-Lⓐⓗ-Dⓤⓗ

church die Kirche DⒺ KⒺR-ᔆᴴⓤⓗ

cigar die Zigarre DⒺ TSⒺⒺ-Gⓐⓗ-Bⓤⓗ

cigarette die Zigarette DⒺ TSⒺⒺ-Gⓐⓗ-BⒺ-Tⓤⓗ

city die Stadt DⒺ SHTⓐⓗT

clean rein BⒾN

close (to) nahe Nⓐⓗ-Hⓤⓗ

closed zu TSⓄⓄ

clothes die Kleider DⒺ KLⒾ-DⓄr

cocktail der Cocktail DⒺR KⓐⓗK-TⒶL

coffee der Kaffee D®R K@h-F@

cold (temperature) kalt K@hLT

comb der Kamm D®R K@hM

come (to) kommen K@-M®N

company (business) das Geschäft D@hS G®-SH®FT

computer der Computer D®R K@M-P®w-T@r

concert das Konzert D@hS K@N-TS®BT

condom das Kondom D@hS K@N-D@M

conference die Konferenz D® K@N-F®-B®NTS

conference room die Konferenzraum

   D® K@N-F®-B®NTS-B@wM

congratulations Gratulierungen

   GR@h-T@@-L®R-@w-N-G®N

copy machine die Kopiermaschine

   D® K@-P®'-@r-M@h-SH®-N@h

corn der Mais D®R M@S

cough medicine der Hustenmittel

   D®R H@@S-T®N-M@-T®L

cover charge die Gebühr D® G®-B®wR

crab die Krabbe D® KR@h-B@h

cream die Sahne D® Z@h-N@h

credit card die Kreditkarte

    DEE KRE-DEET-KahR-Tuh

cup die Tasse DEE Tah-Suh

customs der Zoll DeR TSOL

D

dance (to) tanzen TahN-SeN

dangerous gefährlich GE-FeR-LISH

date (calender) das Datum DahS Dah-TooM

day der Tag DeR TahK

December der Dezember DeR DA-TSeMBUr

delicious köstlich KUST-LIK

delighted entzückt eNT-TSewKT

dentist der Zahnarzt DeR TSahN-ahRTST

deodorant das Deodorant

    DahS DA-O-DO-RahNT

department store das Kaufhaus DahS KahF-HowS

departure die Abfahrt DEE ahP-FahRT

dessert der Nachtisch DeR NahK-TISH

detour der Umweg DeR ooM-VeK

diabetic Zuckerkrank TSou-KUr-KBahNK

diarrhea der Durchfall DeR DooRSH-FahL

dictionary das Wörterbuch DahS VUr-TUr-BooK

dining room das Esszimmer DahS ĕS-TSĬ-MUr

dinner das Abendessen DahS ah-BĔNT-ĕS-ĕN

direction die Richtung DEE RĬSH-TᴀNG

dirty schmutzig SHMᴏŏ-TSĬK

disabled behindert Bĕ-HĬN-DĕRT

discount der Rabatt DĕR Bah-BahT

distance die Distanz DEE DĕS-TahNTS

doctor der Arzt DĕR ahRTST

document die Dokumente DEE DŌ-Kᴏᴏ-MĕN-Tᴜh

dollar der Dollar DĕR Dah-LUr

down unten ᴏᴏN-TᴇN

downtown in der Stadt ĬN DĕR SHTahT

dress das Kleid DahS KLĬT

drink trinken TBĔNK-ĕN

drive (to) fahren FahB-ĕN

drugstore die Drogerie DEE DBŌ-Gĕ-BEE

dry cleaner die Reinigung DEE BĬ-NEE-GᴏᴏNG

duck die Ente DEE ĕN-Tᴜh

E

ear das Ohr DahS ŌR

ear drops die Ohrentropfen

DEE Ō-BĕN-TBŌP-FĕN

early früh FR-ew

east der Osten D(e)R O'ST-(e)N

easy einfach I'N-F(ah)K

eat (to) essen (e)S-(e)N

eggs die Eier D(ee) I'-(Ur)

eggs (fried) die Spiegeleier D(ee) SHP(ee)-G(e)L-I-(Ur)

eggs (scrambled) die Rühreier D(ee) R(oo)R-I-(Ur)

electricity die Elektrizität

　　D(ee) (A)-L(e)K-TR(ee)T-S(ee)-T(A)'T

elevator der Lift D(e)R L(I)FT

embassy die Botschaft D(ee) B(O)T-SH(ah)FT

emergency der Notfall D(e)R N(O)T-F(ah)L

England England (e)N-GL(ah)ND

English der Engländer (m) D(e)R (e)N-GL(uh)N-D(uh)

　　die Engländerin D(ee) (e)N-GL(uh)N-D(e)-R(e)N

English Englisch (e)N-GL(I)SH

enough genug G(e)'-N(oo)K

entrance der Eingang D(e)R I'N-G(ah)NG

envelope der Umschlag D(e)R (ow)M-SHL(ah)K

evening der Abend D(e)R (ah)'-B(e)NT

everything alles (ah)'-L(e)S

excellent ausgezeichnet (ow)'S-G(e)-TS(I)K-N(e)T

excuse me Entschuldigung

ĕNT-SHOOL-DEE-ouNG

exit der Ausgang DĕR owS-GahNG

expensive teuer Toy-Ur

eyes die Augen DEE ow-GĕN

eyedrops die Augentropfen

DEE ow-GĕN-TROP-FĕN

F

face das Gesicht DahS Gĕ-ZEESHT

far weit VIT

fare (cost) der Fahrpreis DĕR FahR-PRIS

fast schnell SHNĕL

fax machine die Faxmaschine

DEE FahKS-Mah-SHEE-Nuh

February der Februar DĕR FA-BRoo-ahR

few wenige VA-NI-Guh

film (movie) das Kino DahS KEE-NO

film (camera) der Film DĕR FILM

fine / very well gut, danke GooT DahN-Kuh

finger der Finger DĕR FEEN-GUr

fire das Feuer DahS Foy-Ur

fire extinguisher der Feuerlöscher

DⓔR Fⓞy´-ⓤr-Lⓤr-SHⓤr

first zuerst TSⓞⓞ´-ⓔRST

fish der Fisch DⓔR FⓘSH

flight der Flug DⓔR FLⓞⓞK

florist shop das Blumengeschäft

DⓐS BLⓞⓞ´-MⓔN-Gⓔ-SHⓔFT

flower die Blume Dⓔⓔ BLⓞⓞ´-Mⓤh

food das Essen DⓐS ⓔ´S-ⓔN

foot der Fuss DⓔR FⓞⓞS

fork die Gabel Dⓔⓔ Gⓐh´-BⓔL

french fries die Pommes Frites Dⓔⓔ PⓄM FRⓔⓔT

fresh frisch FRⓘSH

Friday der Freitag DⓔR FRⓘ´-TⓐhG

fried gebraten Gⓔ-BRⓐhT-TⓔN

friend der Freund DⓔR FRⓞyNT

fruit das Obst DⓐS ⓄBST

funny lustig Lⓤⓤ´S-TⓘG

G

gas station die Tankstelle Dⓔⓔ TⓐNK-SHTⓔ-Lⓤh

gasoline das Benzin DⓐS BⓔN-TSⓔⓔN

gate das Tor DⓐS TⓄR

gentleman der Herr D◎R H◎R

gift das Geschenk D◎S G◎-SH◎NK

girl das Mädchen D◎S M◎D-SH◎N

glass (drinking) das Glas D◎S GL◎S

glasses (eye) die Brille D◎ BR◎-L◎

glove der Handschuh D◎R H◎NT-SH◎

go gehen G◎-◎N

gold (color) das Gold D◎S G◎LD

golf der Golf D◎R G◎LF

golf course der Golfplatz D◎R G◎LF-PL◎TS

good gut G◎T

good-bye auf Wiedersehen ◎F V◎-D◎-Z◎N

goose die Gans D◎ G◎NS

grapes die Trauben D◎ TR◎-B◎N

grateful dankbar D◎NK-B◎R

gray grau GR◎

green grün GR◎N

grocery store das Lebensmittelgeschäft

    D◎S L◎-B◎NZ-M◎-T◎L-G◎-SH◎FT

group die Gruppe D◎ GR◎P-◎

guide der Leiter D◎R L◎-T◎

H

hair die Haare   DⒺⒺ HⓐĦ-Ⓑⓤħ

hairbrush die Haarbürste   DⒺⒺ HⓐR-BⒺⓌR-STⓤħ

haircut der Haarschnitt   DⒺR-HⓐR-SHNⓄT

ham der Schinken   DⒺR SHⒺⒺNK-ⓔN

hamburger der Hamburger   DⒺR HⓐM-Bⓤ-GⓤR

hand die Hand   DⒺⒺ HⓐNT

happy glücklich GLⓔⓌK-LⓄSH

have (I) ich habe ⓄSH̲ HⓐĦ-Bⓤħ

he er ⒺR

head der Kopf DⒺR KⓄPF

headache Kopfschmerzen KⓄPF-SHMⒺRTS-ⓔN

health club das Fitnesstudio

   DⓐS FⓄT-NⒺS SHTⓄⓄ-DⒺⒺ-Ⓞ

heart das Herz DⓐS HⒺRTS

heart condition die Herzkrankheit

   DⒺⒺ HⒺRTS-KⒷⓐNK-HⓄT

heat die Hitze DⒺⒺ HⓄ-TSⓤħ

hello hallo HⓐĦ-LⓄ

help! Hilfe! HⒺⒺL-Fⓤħ

here hier HⒺⒺR

holiday der Feiertag DⒺR FⓄR-TⓐK

hospital das Krankenhaus

    DaS KRaNK-eN-HowS

hot dog die Würstel DEE VewRS-TeL

hotel das Hotel DaS HO-TeL

hour die Stunde DEE SHTouN-Duh

how wie VEE

hurry (to) eilen I-LeN

I

I ich ISH

ice das Eis DaS IS

ice cream das Eis DaS IS

ice cubes die Eiswürfel DEE IS-VewR-FeL

ill krank KRaNK

important wichtig VISH-TIG

indigestion die Verdauungsstörung

    DEE FeR-Dow-ooNG-SHTUr-ooNG

information die Auskunft DEE owS-KooNFT

inn das Gasthaus DaS GaST-HowS

interpreter der Übersetzer

    DeR ew-BeR-ZeT-SUr

J

jacket die Jacke DEE Ya-Kuh

jam die Marmelade   D㋐   M㋐ℝ-M㋐-L㋐́-D㋔

January der Januar   D㋐R   Y㋐́-N㏇-㋐ℝ

jewelry der Schmuck   D㋐R   SHM㏇K

jewelry store das Juweliergeschäft

   D㋐S   Y㏇-V㋐-L㋐́R-G㋐-SH㋐FT

job der Job   D㋐R   J㋐B

juice der Saft   D㋐R   Z㋐FT

July der Juli   D㋐R   Y㏇-L㋐

June der Juni   Y㏇-N㋐

K

ketchup der Ketschup   D㋐R   K㋐T-CH㋔P

key der Schlüssel   D㋐R   SHL㋔L-S㋐L

kiss der Kuß   D㋐R   K㋖S

knife das Messer   D㋐S   M㋐́-S㋖

know (I) ich kenne   ㋑SH   K㋐-N㋔

L

Ladies (restroom) Damen   D㋐́-M㋐N

lady die Dame   D㋐   D㋐́-M㋔

lamb das Lamm   D㋐S   L㋔M

language die Sprache   D㋐   SHPR㋐́-K㋔

large groß   GR㋔S

late spät SHP(A)T

laundry die Wäsche D(EE) V(ĕ)-SH(uh)

lawyer der Rechtsanwalt D(ĕ)R R(ĕ)SHTS-(ah)N-V(ah)LT

left (direction) links L(EE)NKS

leg das Bein D(ah)S B(I)N

lemon die Zitrone D(EE) TS(i)-TR(O)-N(uh)

less weniger V(A)-N(i)-G(Ur)

letter der Brief D(ĕ)R BR(EE)F

lettuce der Salat D(ĕ)R Z(ah)-L(ah)T

light das Licht D(ah)S L(i)SHT

like (I) ich habe...gerne (I)SH H(ah)-B(uh)...G(ĕ)R-N(uh)

like (I would) ich möchte (I)SH M(Ur)SH-T(uh)

lip die Lippen D(EE) L(i)-P(ĕ)N

lipstick der Lippenstift D(ĕ)R L(i)-P(ĕ)N-SHT(i)FT

little (size) klein KL(I)N

little (amount) ein wenig (I)N V(A)-N(i)G

live (to) leben L(A)-B(ĕ)N

lobster der Hummer D(ĕ)R H(oo)-M(Ur)

long lang L(ah)NG

lost verloren F(ĕ)R-L(O)-R(ĕ)N

love lieben L(EE)-B(ĕ)N

luck das Glück D@hS GL@K

luggage das Gepäck D@hS G@-P@K

lunch das Mittagessen D@hS M@-T@hK-@S-@N

M

maid das Zimmermädchen

   D@hS TS@-M@r-M@D-CH@N

mail die Post D@ P@ST

makeup die Schminke D@ SHM@N-K@h

man der Mann D@R   M@hN

manager der Chef D@R SH@F

map die Karte D@ K@hR-T@h

March der März D@R M@RTS

market der Markt D@R M@hRKT

matches die Streichhölzer D@ STR@CH-H@L-TS@r

May der Mai D@R M@

mayonnaise die Mayonnaise D@ M@-@-N@-Z@h

meal die Mahlzeit D@ M@hL-TS@T

meat das Fleisch D@hS FL@SH

mechanic der Mechaniker D@R M@-K@h-N@-K@r

medicine die Medizin D@ M@-D@-TS@N

meeting die Treffung D@ TR@-F@NG

Mens' (restroom) Herren H&R-@N

menu die Speisekarte / das Menu

D& SP①-Z@-K@R-T@ / D@S M&-N@

message die Botschaft D& B⊙T-SH@FT

milk die Milch D& M⊙L<u>SH</u>

mineral water das Mineralwasser

D@S M&-N&-R@L-V@-S⊕r

minute die Minute D& M①-N@-T@

Miss Fräulein FR@y-L①N

mistake der Fehler D&R F@-L⊕r

misunderstanding das Mißverständnis

D@S M①S-F&R-SHT&ND-N①S

moment der Moment D&R M⊙-M&NT

Monday der Montag D&R M⊙N-T@G

money das Geld D@S G&LD

month der Monat D&R M⊙-N@T

monument das Denkmal D@S D&NK-M@L

more mehr M&R

morning der Morgen D&R M⊙R-G&N

mosque die Moschee D& M⊙-SH@

mother die Mutter D& M@-T@

mountain der Berg D&R B&RG

movies das Kino D@hS K㉫-N⓪

Mr. Herr H㊚R

Mrs. Frau FR⓪ⓌⓌ

much (too) zu viel TS⓪⓪ F㉫L

museum das Museum D@hS M⓪⓪-Z④-⓪ⓊM

mushrooms die Pilze D㉫ P㊀L-TS⓾

music die Musik D㉫ M⓪⓪-Z㉫K

mustard der Senf D㊚R Z㊚NF

N

nail polish der Nagellack D㊚R N@h-G㉫L-L@hK

name der Name D㊚R N@h-M⓾

napkin die Serviette D㉫ S㊚R-V㉫-④-T⓾

near nahe N@h-H⓾

neck der Hals D㊚R H@hLTS

need (I) ich brauche ㊀ᔆᴴ BR⓪Ⓦ-K⓾

never niemals N㉫-M@hLS

newspaper die Zeitung D㉫ TS㊀-T⓾NG

news stand der Kiosk D㊚R K㉫-@hᔆK

next time nächstes Mal N㊚KS-T㊚S M@hL

night die Nacht D㉫-N@hKT

nightclub das Nachtlokal D@hS N@hKT-L⓪-K@hL

no nein NⒾN

no smoking rauchen verboten

Rⓦ-KⓔN FⒺR-BⓄ-TⓔN

noon der Mittag DⒺR MⒾ-TⓐG

north der Norden DⒺR NⓄRD-ⓔN

notary der Notar DⒺR NⓄ-TⓐR

November der November DⒺR NⓄ-VⓔM-BⓊr

now jetzt YⓔTST

number die Nummer DⒺⒺ NⓄⓄ-MⓊr

nurse die Krankenschwester

DⒺⒺ KRⓐNK-ⓔN-SHVⓔS-TⓊr

O

occupied besetzt Bⓔ-ZⓔTST

ocean das Meer DⓐS MⒶR

October der Oktober DⒺR ⓄK-TⓄ-BⓊr

officer der Offizier DⒺR Ⓞ-Fⓘ-TSⒺR

oil das öl DⓐS ⓊL

omelet die Omelette DⒺⒺ ⓄM-Lⓔ-Tⓤh

one-way (traffic) die Einbahnstraße

DⒺⒺ ⓘN-BⓐN-SHTRⓐ-Sⓤh

onion die Zwiebel DⒺⒺ TSVⒺⒺ-BⓔL

open (to) aufmachen ⓪F-Mah K-ⓔN

opera die Oper Dⓔⓔ ⓪-Pⓤr

operator der Telefonist DⓔR Tⓔ-Lⓔ-Fⓞ N-ⓘST

optician der Optiker DⓔR ⓞP-Tⓘ-Kⓤr

orange (color) orangen ⓞ-Rah N-ZHⓔN

orange (fruit) die Orange Dⓔⓔ ⓞ-Rah N-ZHuh

order (to) bestellen Bⓔ-SHTⓔ-LⓔN

original originell ⓞ-Rⓘ-Gⓘ-Nⓔ L

owner der Eigentümer DⓔR ⓘ-GⓔN-Tew-Mⓤr

oysters die Austern Dⓔⓔ ⓞw-STⓤrN

P

package das Paket Dah S Pah-Kⓐ T

paid bezahlt Bⓔ-TSah LT

pain der Schmerz DⓔR SHMⓔRTS

painting das Gemälde Dah S GⓔM-ah L-Dⓔ

pantyhose die Strümpfe Dⓔⓔ SHTRew MP-Fuh

paper das Papier Dah S Pah-PⓔⓔR

park (to) parken Pah RK-ⓔN

partner (business) der Partner DⓔR Pah RT-Nⓤr

party die Party Dⓔⓔ Pah R-Tⓔⓔ

passenger der Passagier DⓔR Pah-Sah-GⓔⓔR

passport der Pass DÊR PahS

pasta die Pasta DEE PahS-Tah

pastry der Teig DÊR TIG

pen der Kuli DÊR KOO-LEE

pencil der Bleistift DÊR BLI-SHTIFT

pepper der Pfeffer DÊR PFÊ-FUr

perfume das Parfüme DahS PahR-FewM

person die Person DEE PÊR-ZON

person to person (telephone) Person an Person

PÊR-ZON ahN PÊR-ZON

pharmacist der Apotheker DÊR ah-PO-TA-KUr

pharmacy die Apotheke DEE ah-PO-TA-Kuh

phone book das Telefonbuch

DahS TÊ-LÊ-FON-BooK

photo das Photo DahS FO-TO

photographer der Photograph

DÊR FO-TO-GRah-Fuh

pie die Pastete DEE PahS-STA-Tuh

pillow das Kissen DahS KIS-ÊN

pink rosa RO-Zah

pizza die Pizza DEE PEET-Sah or PEE-Sah

plate der Teller DⒺR TⒺ-LⓊr

please bitte BⒾ-Tⓤh

pleasure die Vergnügeng DⒺⒺ FⒺR-GNⓔⓦ-GⓊhNG

police die Polizei DⒺⒺ PⓄ-LⒾ-TSⒾ

police station die Polizeistation

DⒺⒺ PⓄ-LⒾ-TSⒾ-STⓐh-TSⒺⒺ-ⓄN

pork das Schweinefleisch DⓐhS SHVⒾ-Nⓤh-FLⒾSH

porter der Hausdiener DⒺR HⓄⓦS-DⒺⒺ-NⓊr

post office das Postamt DⓐhS PⓄ́ST-ⓐhMT

postcard das Postkarte DⓐhS PⓄ́ST-KⓐhR-Tⓤh

potato die Kartoffel DⒺⒺ KⓐhR-TⓄ́-FⒺ̲L

pregnant schwanger SHVⓐhN-GⓊr

prescription das Rezept DⓐhS RⒺ-TSⒺ́PT

price der Preis DⒺR PRⒾS

problem das Problem DⓐhS PRⓄ-BLⓐM

profession der Beruf DⒺR BⒶ-RⓄⓞF

public öffentlich Ⓤr-FⒺNT-LⒾ<u>SH</u>

public telephone das öffentliche Telefon

DⓐhS Ⓤr-FⒺNT-LⒾ-<u>SH</u>ⓤh TⒺ-LⒺ-FⓄ́N

purified gereinigt GⒺ-RⒾ-NⒾKT

purple lila LⒺⒺ-Lⓐh

purse die Handtasche DEE HahNT-Tah-SHuh

Q

quality die Qualität DEE KVah-LEE-TAT

question die Frage DEE FRah-Guh

quickly schnell SHNeL

quiet ruhe ROO-Huh

quiet (to be) ruhe sein ROO-Huh SIN

R

radio das Radio DahS Bah-DEE-O

railroad die Bahn DEE BahN

rain der Regen DeR Ba-GeN

raincoat der Regenmantel

DeR Ba-GeN-Mahn-TeL

ramp die Rampe DEE BahM-Puh

rare (steak) blutig BLOO-TiK

razor blades die Rasierklingen

DEE Bah-ZeR-KLEENG-eN

ready fertig FeR-TiK

receipt die Quittung DEE KVi-TowNG

recommend (to) empfehlen eMP-Fa-LeN

red rot ⓡⓄT

repeat wiederholen ⓋⓔⒺ-Ⓓⓤⓡ-ⒽⓄ-Lⓔ̈N

reservation die Reservierung

   ⒹⓔⒺ ⓡⓔ̈-Sⓔ̈R-ⓋⓔⒺⓡ-ⓄⓊNG

restaurant das Restaurant Ⓓⓐⓗ ⓡⓔ̈S-TⓄ-ⓡⓐⓗNT

return (to come back) zurückkehren

   TSⓄⓄ-ⓡⓔⓦK-Kⓔ̈R-ⓔ̈N

return (to give back) zurückgeben

   TSⓄⓄ-ⓡⓔⓦK-GⓐⒶ-Bⓔ̈N

rice der Reis Dⓔ̈ⓡ ⓡⓄS

rich reich ⓡⓄ̈sh

right (correct) richtig ⓡⓄ̈SH-TⓄG

right (direction) nach rechts NⓐⓗK ⓡⓔⒺSHTS

road die Straße DⓔⒺ STHRⓐⓗ-Sⓤⓗ

room das Zimmer DⓐⓗS TSⓄ̈-Mⓤⓡ

round trip die Rundfahrt DⓔⒺ ⓡⓄⓤNT-FⓐⓗRT

S

safe (box) das Tresor DⓐⓗS TRⓔ̈-ZⓄⓡ

salad der Salat Dⓔ̈ⓡ Zⓐⓗ-Lⓐⓗ̈T

sale das Sonderangebot

   DⓐⓗS ZⓄ̈N-Dⓤⓡ-ⓐⓗN-Gⓤⓗ-BⓄⓄT

salmon der Lachs DÊR LahKS

salt das Salz DahS ZahLTS

sandwich das Belegte Brot

   DahS BÊ-LAK-Tuh BROT

Saturday der Samstag DÊR ZahMS-TahG

scissors die Schere DEE SHÊR-uh

sculpture die Skulptur DEE SKooLP-TooR

seafood die Meeresfrüchte

   DEE MA-RÊS-FRoo-SHTuh

season die Jahreszeit DEE YahR-uhS-TSIT

seat der Sitz DÊR ZITS

secretary die Sekretärin (f) der Sekretär (m)

   DEE SÊK-RÊ-TÊR-IN / DÊR SÊK-RÊ-TÊR

section die Sektion DEE SÊK-TSEE-ON

September der September DÊR ZÊP-TÊM-BUR

service der Dienst DÊR DEENST

several ein paar IN PahR

shampoo das Shampoo DahS SHahM-Poo

sheets (bed) die Leintücher DEE LIN-Tew-SHUr

shirt das Hemd DahS HÊMT

shoe der Schuh DÊR SHoo

shoe store der Schuhladen　DⒺR　SHⓄⓄ-Lⓐ-DⒺN

shop　der Laden　DⒺR　Lⓐ-DⒺN

shopping center　das Einkaufszentrum

　　　Dⓐs　ⒾN-KⓄⓌF-TSⒺN-TRⓄM

shower die Dusche　DⒺ　DⓄⓄ-SHⓊ

shrimp die Garnele　DⒺ　Gⓐ R-NⒺ-LⓊ

sick krank　KRⓐNK

sign (display) das Schild　Dⓐs　SHⒺLD

signature die Unterschrift

　　　DⒺ　ⓊN-TⓊ-SHRⒾFT

single ledig　LⒶ-DⒾK

sir mein Herr　MⒾN　HⒺR

sister die Schwester　DⒺ　SHVⒺS-TⓊ

size die Grösse　DⒺ　GRⓊ-SⓊ

skin die Haut　DⒺ　HⓄⓌT

skirt der Rock　DⒺR　ROK

sleeve der Ärmel　DⒺR　ⒺR-MⒺL

slowly langsam　Lⓐ NG-Kⓐ M

small klein　KLⒾN

smile (to) lächeln　LⒺ-KⒺLN

smoke (to) rauchen　RⓄⓌ-KⒺN

soap die Seife DEE ZÏ-Fuh

sock der Sock DèR ZOK

some einige Ï-NÏ-Guh

something etwas èT-VahS

sometimes manchmal MahNK-MahL

soon bald BahLT

sorry (I am) es tut mir leid èS TooT MEER LÏT

soup die Suppe DEE ZoU-Puh

south der Süden DèR ZOO-DèN

souvenir das Andenken DahS ahN-DèN-KÈN

specialty die Spezialität DEE SPè-TSEE-ah-LÏ-TÄT

speed die Geschwindigkeit

   DEE Gè-SHVÏN-DÏ-KÏT

spoon der Löffel DèR LÜ-FÈL

sport der Sport DèR SHPORT

spring (season) der Frühling DèR FRew-LEENG

stairs die Treppen DEE TRè-PèN

stamp die Briefmarke DEE BREEF-MahR-Kuh

station die Station DEE SHTahT-SEE-ON

steak das Steak DahS SHTAK

steamed gedünstet Gè-DouNST-èD

Stop! Halt! H@LT

store das Geschäft D@S G@-SH@FT

storm der Sturm D@R SHT@RM

straight ahead geradeaus G@-R@-D@h-@wS

strawberry die Erdbeere D@ @RT-B@R-@h

street die Straße D@ SHTR@-S@h

string der Faden D@R F@-D@N

subway die U-bahn D@ @-B@N

sugar der Zucker D@R TS@K@r

suit (clothes) der Anzug D@R @N-TS@K

suitcase der Koffer D@R K@-F@r

summer der Sommer D@R Z@-M@r

sun die Sonne D@ Z@-N@h

sunglasses die Sonnenbrille

  D@ Z@-N@N-BR@-L@h

suntan lotion die Sonnenschutzcreme

  D@ Z@-N@N-SH@TS-KR@-M@h

Sunday der Sonntag D@R Z@N-T@G

supermarket der Supermarkt Z@-P@R-M@RKT

surprise die Überraschung D@ @-B@R-R@-SH@NG

sweet süß Z@S

swim (to) schwimmen SHVİ-MℯN

swimming pool das Schwimmbad

　　DℯS SHVİM-BℯT

synagogue die Synagoge DÉE Zℯ-Nℯ-GÓ-Guh

T

table der Tisch DℯR Tİ<u>SH</u>

tampon der Tampon DℯR TℯM-PÓN

tape (sticky) der Tesefilm DℯR TÁ-Zuh-Fİ LM

tape recorder der Kassettenrekorder

　　DℯR Kℯ-SÉ-TℯN-RÉ-KÓR-DUr

tax die Steuer DÉE SHToy-Ur

taxi das Taxi DℯS Tℯ́K-SÉE

tea der Tee DℯR TÁ

telegram das Telegramm DℯS TÉ-LÉ-GRℯM

telephone das Telefon DℯS TÉ-LÉ-FÓN

television der Fernseher DℯR FÉRN-ZÁ-Ur

temperature die Temperatur DÉE TÉM-PUr-ℯ-TooR

temple der Temple DÉE TÉMPL

tennis das Tennis DℯS TÉ-Nİ́S

tennis court der Tennisplatz DℯR TÉ-Nİ S-PLℯTS

thank you danke schön DℯN-Kuh SHUℯN

that das D@hS

the der (m) / die (f) / das (neuter) / die (plural)

　　D@R　/　D@　/　D@hS　/　D@

theater das Theater D@hS T@-@h-TR@r

there dort D@RT

they sie Z@

this dieser (m) / diese (f) / dieses (n) / diese (pl)

　　D@-Z@r　/　D@-Z@h　/　D@-Z@S　/　D@-Z@h

thread der Faden D@R F@h-D@N

throat der Hals D@R H@hLS

Thursday der Donnerstag D@R D@-N@r-ST@hG

ticket das Ticket / die Karte

　　D@hS T@-K@T　/　D@ K@hR-T@h

tie die Krawatte D@ KR@h-V@h-T@h

time die Zeit D@ TS@T

tip (gratuity) das Trinkgeld D@hS TR@NK-G@LT

tire (car) der Reifen D@R R@-F@N

tired müde M@-D@h

toast der Toast D@R T@ST

tobacco der Tabak D@R T@h-B@hK

today heute H@Y-T@h

toe die Zehe DEE TSA-uh

together zusammen TSoo-Zah-MEN

toilet die Toilette / das Klo

DEE TWah-LET / DahS KLO

toilet paper das Toilettenpapier

DahS TWah-LE-TEN-Pah-PEER

tomato die Tomate DEE TO-Mah-Tuh

tomorrow morgen MOR-GEN

toothache das Zahnweh DahS TSahN-VA

toothbrush die Zahnbürste DEE TSahN-BewRS-Tuh

toothpaste die Zahnpaste DEE TSahN-PahS-Tuh

toothpick der Zahnstocher DER TSahN-SHTO-KUr

tour die Tour DEE TooR

tourist der Tourist DER TooR-OST

tourist office das Reisebüro DahS RO-Zuh-Bew-RO

towel das Handtuch DahS HahN-TooK

train der Zug DER TSooG

travel agency das Reisebüro

DahS RO-Zuh-Bew-RO

traveler's checks die Reiseschecks

DEE RO-Zuh-SHEKS

trip die Reise DⒺ BⓎ-Zⓞ

trousers die Hose DⒺ HⓄ-Zⓞ

trout die Forelle DⒺ FⓄ-Rⓔ-Lⓞ

truth die Wahrheit DⒺ VⓐR-HⓎT

Tuesday der Dienstag DⓔR DⒺNS-TⓐG

turkey der Truthahn DⓔR TRⓛT-HⓐN

U

umbrella der Regenschirm DⓔR Rⓐ-GⓔN-SHⓔRM

understand (to) verstehen FⓔR-SHTⓐ-ⓔN

underwear die Unterwäsche DⒺ ⓞN-TⓔR-Vⓔ-SHⓞ

United Kingdom das Vereinigte Königreich
    DⓐS FⓔR-Ⓨ-NⓎK-Tⓞ Kⓛ-NⓎK-RⓎK

United States die Vereinigten Staaten
    DⒺ FⓔR-Ⓨ-NⓎK-TⓔN SHTⓐ-TⓔN

university die Universität DⒺ ⓛ-NⒺ-VⓔR-ZⒺ-TⓐT

up oben Ⓞ-BⓔN

urgent drigend DRⒺN-GⓔNT

V

vacancies (accommodation) Zimmer frei
    TSⓎ-Mⓞr FBⓎ

vacant frei FBⓎ

vacation die Ferien D︎EE F︎ĒR-EE-︎ēN

valuable wertvoll V︎ĒRT-F︎OL

value der Wert D︎ēR V︎ĒRT

vanilla die Vanille D︎EE V︎ah-N︎EE-L︎uh

veal das Kalbfleisch D︎ahS K︎ahLB-FL︎ISH

vegetables das Gemüse D︎ahS G︎ē-M︎ew-Z︎uh

view die Aussicht D︎EE ︎owS-Z︎I^SH^T

vinegar der Essig D︎ēR ︎ē-S︎IG

voyage die Reise D︎EE R︎I-Z︎uh

W

wait! Warte! V︎ahR-T︎uh

waiter der Kellner D︎ēR K︎ēL-N︎Ur

waitress die Kellnerin D︎EE K︎ēL-N︎Ur-︎IN

want (I) ich möchte ︎I^SH^ M︎Ur^SH^-T︎uh

wash (to) washen V︎ah-SH︎ēN

watch (timepiece) die Uhr D︎EE ︎ooR

Watch out! Achtung! ︎ahK-T︎ooNG

water das Wasser D︎ahS V︎ah-S︎Ur

water (drinking) das Leitungswasser

  D︎ahS L︎I-T︎ooNGS V︎ah-S︎Ur

watermelon die Wassermelone

　　DEE VAH-SUr-MEE-LO-Nuh

we wir VEER

weather das Wetter DAHS VE-TUr

Wednesday der Mittwoch DER MIT-VOK

week die Woche DEE VO-Kuh

weekend das Wochenende DAHS VO-KEN-EN-Duh

welcome willkommen VEL-KO-MEN

well done (food) gut durchbraten

　　GOOT DOORK-BRAH-TEN

west der Westen DER VES-TEN

What? Was? VAHS

wheelchair der Rollstuhl DER ROL-SHTOOL

When? Wann? VAHN

Where? Wo? VO

Which? Welche? / Welcher? / Welches?

　　VEL-SHuh / VEL-SHUr / VEL-CHES

white weiß VIS

Who? Wer? VER

why? Warum? VAH-ROOM

wife die Frau DEE FROW

wind der Wind D@R V①NT

window das Fenster D@hS F@N-ST@r

wine der Wein D@R V①N

wine list die Weinliste D@ V①N-L①S-T@h

winter der Winter D@R V①N-T@r

with mit M①T

woman die Frau D@ FR@w

wonderful wunderbar V@N-D@R-B@hR

world die Welt D@ V@LT

wrong (incorrect) falsch F@hLSH

XYZ

year das Jahr D@hS Y@hR

yellow gelb G@LB

yes ja Y@h

yesterday gestern G@-ST@N

you Sie (formal) / sie (Plural) / du (informal)

    Z@ / D@

zipper der Reißverschluss

    D@R B①S-F@R-SHL@S

zoo der Zoo D@R TS@

THANKS!

The nicest thing you can say to anyone in any language is "Thank you." Try some of these languages using the incredible EPLS Vowel Symbol System.

Spanish	French
GR(ah)́-S(EE)-(ah)S	M(ĕ)R-S(EE)

German	Italian
D(ah)́N-K(uh)	GR(ah)́T-S(EE)-(ĕ)

Japanese	Chinese
D(o)-M(o)	SH(EE)(ĕ) SH(EE)(ĕ)

Swedish	Portuguese
TⓐK	Ⓞ-BⓇⒺ-Gⓐ́-DⓄ

Arabic	Greek
SHⓄⓄ-KⓇⓐN	ⓔ́F-Hⓐ-BⒺ-STⓄ́

Hebrew	Russian
TⓄ-Dⓐ́	SPⓐ-SⒺ-Bⓐ

Swahili	Dutch
ⓐ-Sⓐ́N-TⒶ	Dⓐ́NK ⓄⓄ

Tagalog	Hawaiian
Sⓐ-Lⓐ-Mⓐ́T	Mⓐ-Hⓐ́-LⓄ

INDEX

NOTES

QUICK REFERENCE PAGE

Hello

Guten Tag

GOO-TEN TahK

Good-bye

Auf wiedersehen

OWF VEE-DUr-ZAN

How are you?

Wie geht es Ihnen?

VEE GAT eS EE-NEN

Fine / Very well

Sehr gut

ZER GOOT

Yes

Ja

Yah

No

Nein

NIN

Please

Bitte

BI-Tuh

Thank you

Danke schön

DahN-Kuh SHUrN

I would like...

Ich möchte...

ISH MUrSH-Tuh...

Where is...

Wo is...

VO IST...

I don't understand!

Ich verstehe nicht!

ISH FER-SHTA-uh NISHT

Help!

Hilfe!

HEEL-Fuh

166